*Twayne's United States Authors Series*

Sylvia E. Bowman, *Editor*

INDIANA UNIVERSITY

*John Woolman*

# JOHN WOOLMAN

By PAUL ROSENBLATT

*University of Arizona*

 147

Twayne Publishers, Inc.　::　New York

50023

FOR JOAN

# Preface

WITH THE POSSIBLE EXCEPTION of Benjamin Franklin, John Woolman is to us the most modern of our colonial writers. Yet his *Journal* has as much in common with *The Confessions of St. Augustine* and *The Imitation of Christ* as with any clearly American book. To know the life and writings of John Woolman is to be haunted forever by the mystery of the endless dimensions of love. Indeed, Woolman's writings have been generously studied for inspiration and devotion; and it is not uncommon for a young Quaker to receive as a graduation gift, along with the Bible, a copy of Woolman's *Journal*. But, as all the world knows (I presume), Quaker inspiration and devotion have manifested themselves in active, humanitarian responses to the terrifying degradation of war, civil inequality, and poverty. To read Woolman is also to read a meditation, almost chapter and verse, on the headlines of our time.

John Woolman's life has been celebrated by Amelia Mott Gummere in the biographical introduction to her edition of *The Journal and Essays of John Woolman* (1922) and by Janet Whitney in *John Woolman, Quaker* (1943). I have drawn chiefly upon these sources and, of course, the *Journal*, for the details of his life. Woolman's ideas and their relevance to his age and to ours have been most recently and persuasively analyzed by Professor Edwin Cady in his *John Woolman* (1965).

Some readers may feel that my book has placed too heavy a stress—three chapters—on *The Journal of John Woolman;* but my writing has grown out of an increasing conviction that Woolman's *Journal* is a literary masterpiece which, in deriving its power from the rhythms of a spiritual idealism wholly committed to the radical energies of its culture, has become an authentic American voice. I have spent some time, therefore, in relating Woolman to his culture and to his great contemporaries, Franklin and Jonathan Edwards, who, in the humane practicality of the one and the spiritual idealism of the other, are generally considered representatives of the temper and thought of our colonial period. To a much lesser degree, I have also compared Woolman to Emerson,

Thoreau, and Whitman because I feel these comparisons are relevant to our historical understanding of Woolman's place in the prophetic-radical tradition of American culture.

Since Woolman's beginnings are uniquely Quaker, I have devoted my first chapter to a brief sketch of the rise of The Society of Friends. I end the chapter on a note of conflict; for the Quakers in the Middle Colonies have been caught in a compromise between their faith and their inclination toward worldly riches and power. As we shall see, this conflict constitutes a destiny for John Woolman, who, in leading the Quakers out from the snares of material bondage, became ultimately committed to all people in the hold of the material. Thus, I think of the essential theme of my book as one dealing with modes of liberation, for this *motif* provides us with the various meanings of Woolman's life and work.

In the second chapter, I try to capture through biographical detail and interpretation the emergence of that kind of genius which dwells deeply in life and makes of all that it touches a spiritual experience. Chapters 3 and 4 describe Woolman's apostolicism—his efforts to free the slaves and to maintain peace and equity with the Indians. Chapter 5 stresses his economic views; for, it seems to me, Woolman believed that no resolutions to the problems of peace and war and of slave and Indian were possible unless we recognized that economic considerations were inextricable from moral concerns.

The deepest springs of Woolman's life and thought have gone into the making of his *Journal,* and my hope is that the reader will be oriented for a somewhat extensive analysis of this remarkable work in Chapters 6 through 8. The final chapter of my essay presents Woolman's views on education, for the meaning of his life and writings leads us, in the end, to a quest for values—and, broadly, this quest is what education is about. Values suggest influences, and my closing remarks are in effect a statement of those values I find most enduring in Woolman's work.

One word about my choice of text. I have chosen for study the Gummere edition of *The Journal and Essays of John Woolman* because of its completeness. Mrs. Gummere has not established a definitive text—there is none—but her work offers variant readings and excellent notes which illuminate for us Woolman's manuscripts. All parenthetical references in the body of my text are to the Gummere edition. I have tried to quote generously from the writings of Woolman to give the reader the sense and flavor of his style; and I happily maintained, when quoting, Woolman's spelling and punctuation not so much for reasons of scholarship as for the delights of antiquarian charm.

PAUL ROSENBLATT

*Tucson, Arizona*

# Acknowledgments

I wish to express my gratitude to the Book and Publications Committee, which acts for the Philadelphia Yearly Meeting of the Religious Society of Friends, for granting me permission to quote extensively from Amelia Gummere's *The Journal of John Woolman*. I have mentioned my indebtedness to her work and to Janet Whitney's *John Woolman, Quaker*. Although my essay was well in progress when Edwin Cady's *John Woolman* appeared, I found myself revising in response to the stimulus of his study. The books of the Quaker historians to whom I feel a particular indebtedness appear in the Selected Bibliography section of this book, but I must mention the name of Frederick B. Tolles whose *Meeting House and Counting House: The Quaker Merchants of Colonial Philadelphia, 1682-1763*, helped me, by establishing certain aspects of the essential background of Woolman's milieu, to define the whole intent and direction of my essay.

To Professor Sylvia Bowman I owe a special debt of gratitude. If it were not for her many suggestions for revision and improvement of my manuscript, I should have been loathe to let *John Woolman* see the light. And a final note: my writing has been sustained and encouraged by the critical acuity and good will of my wife Joan.

# Contents

# Contents

# Chronology

1720   John Woolman born October 19, on a plantation in Rancocas, West Jersey, eldest son and fourth child in a family that numbered thirteen children.

1727   Attends village school. Has his first vision of God's purity and sweetness, the first of many "religious" dreams and prophetic visions.

1736-  Falls into wanton company. Patterns of illness and recov-
1740   ery reflect an intense spiritual struggle.

1740-  Leaves plantation to clerk in a shop in Mount Holly. His
1741   first appearance in the ministry.

1743   His ministry recognized and recorded. Gains momentous insight and religious conviction into the evils of slavery. Makes a religious journey, the first of many in a lifetime devoted to the traveling ministry.

1747   Death of his sister Elizabeth.

1748   Opens his own shop in Mount Holly.

1749   Marries Sarah Ellis.

1750   Father, Samuel Woolman, dies. Daughter, Mary, born.

1754   Son, William, three months old, dies. Publishes *Some Considerations on the Keeping of Negroes, Part I.*

1755-  Opposes war tax and draft. Agitates successfully to keep
1757   the Quakers at peace as war comes to Pennsylvania.

1756   Withdraws from business. Begins to write his *Journal.*

1758   Publishes *Considerations on Pure Wisdom and Human Policy.* One of the leaders at the Philadelphia Yearly Meeting where dramatic progress is made to abolish slavery in the Society of Friends.

1760   Serious illness, spiritual struggle, need for further purification, decision to wear undyed clothing.

1762    Publishes *Considerations on the Keeping of Negroes, Part II.*

1763    Writes *A Plea for the Poor* (published 1793).

1765    Teaches school at various intervals during the late 1760's.

1770    Publishes *Considerations on the True Harmony of Mankind.*

1772    Writes *Conversations on the True Harmony of Mankind* (published in 1837). Writes farewell *Epistle* to Friends in America. Voyages to England; account of sea journey and his travels, "last essays." Death at York on October 7.

1774    Joseph Crukshank, Philadelphia printer, publishes The Works of John Woolman: Part I, *The Journal of John Woolman;* Part II, *Other Writings.*

And her ear was pleased with the Thee and Thou of the Quakers,
For it recalled the past, the old Acadian country,
Where all men were equal, and all were brothers and sisters.

—Longfellow, *Evangeline*

CHAPTER *1*

# "A People in White Raimant"

IN 1652, SIXTY-EIGHT years before the birth of John
Woolman, George Fox had a vision atop a "great high hill
called Pendle Hill." There, on the hill facing Lancashire sea, he
prophesied that "a great people" were "to be gathered" and that
they were "a people in white raimant" who "were coming to the
Lord."[1] This prophetic vision on Pendle Hill marks the historical
beginnings of The Society of Friends.[2] The ensuing ministry, as
Fox traveled under incredible conditions of hardship and persecution from place to place gathering disciples, recalls to us the
rhythms of a primitive and apostolic Christianity. Indeed, in one
household Fox visited shortly after his vision, he declared himself
to be the son of God.

## I  *George Fox*

William Penn, in his portrait of Fox, writes that: "The
mystery of the first and second Adam, of the fall and resto-
ration, of the law and gospel, of shadows and substances, of the
servant's and son's state, and the fulfilling of the Scriptures in
Christ and by Christ, the true Light, in all that are His through
the obedience of faith, were much of the substance and drift of
his [Fox's] testimonies. In all which he was witnessed to be of
God, being sensibly felt to speak that which he has received of
Christ and was his own experience, in that which never errs or
fails."[3] Penn's testimony treats Fox "almost as a third Adam," for
Penn saw in the founder of Quakerism the man destined to revive
Christianity to the state of innocence, Adam before the Fall, and
the state of redemptive purity, the coming of Christ, the second
Adam.[4] The apocalyptic fervor of the early days of this "tiny dis-
senting sect" of Quakers involved a tenacious naïveté that they

were "to usher in the final dispensation," the word of the Holy Spirit in man. And yet, because of "the pentecostal atmosphere" of the Quakers, their claim for a spiritual world conquest was made to seem credible—"at least to Quakers like Penn," as Frederick B. Tolles has said.[5]

To understand the essence of this radical departure from established Christianity, we must remember that Quakerism was part of a general history, beginning with the Reformation in the sixteenth century, reducing Christianity to its essentials. The Reformation began with the break from the Papacy, and led inevitably, it would seem, to a reduction in the sacraments of the Church of England, to additional elimination of sacrament and episcopacy in dissenting groups such as the Presbyterians and Independents (Congregationalists), and to still more spontaneous forms of worship in the Baptists who moved so far from all liturgical emphases that they did away with an ordained ministry and relied almost wholly upon "conversion and the gift of the spirit."[6] The Quakers might have indeed believed the final dispensation was at hand; for, under the preaching of George Fox, all sacrament was rejected; and the celebrants in the meeting house, without song or sermon, awaited in silence the leadings of the inner light.

## II  *The Inner Light*

The inner light of the Quakers is the belief that God is immanent in the human heart. This belief formed the central doctrine of Fox's preaching, and, we might say, the only one. Fox preached not an historical but a personal and perpetual revelation of Deity. In rejecting all theological doctrine, he put in place of intellectual dispute the reality of the experience of God in man. Rather than dogma, Fox and his followers offered "testimonies" of experience; and these "testimonies," as they bear witness to the leadings of the Holy Spirit, take on a sacramental nature. The experience of the presence of divinity makes the living of life itself a sacrament. Moreover, the inner light in each man offered possibilities for an intense, self-reliant individualism as the Holy Spirit drew forth the soul and led it into "concerns," while the "testimonies" of individuals furnished the scripture that converted individual into group experience.

[ 22 ]

The inner light was not, however, an exclusive principle of the Quakers. It was advocated as early as 1644 by the General Baptists. William Penn compared "the principle with the 'Great Light' of Pythagoras, the 'divine mind' of Anaxagoras, the Socratic 'good spirit,' Plato's 'perfect principle of truth,' and Plotinus' 'root of the soul.'"[7] It is not to our purpose in this chapter to trace as weighty a subject as "the correspondence between the inner light and the ultimate principle of the ancients,"[8] but that we distinguish the inner light of Quakerism from "the Divine and Supernatural Light" of Calvinism is pertinent for an understanding of the milieu of John Woolman. We may recall that the light of Calvinism could be a rather dim one, indeed, separated from all egalitarian implications; for it flickered with dogmas of predestination, of the elect, of hellfire and damnation. The inner light of the Quakers is to be identified with Christ Himself offering the possibility of salvation to all men.[9]

In discussing Woolman's Puritan contemporary, Jonathan Edwards, Professor Joseph Blau writes that: "The Edwardean divine light was a supplementary sense added to man's natural sense by Divine Grace, as a formulation for man's ideas of divinity. The Quaker inner light was a specific and direct guidance from God to prompt man to particular actions in any situation, and therefore a foundation for man's humanity."[10] Edwards thought of the supernatural light as the light of illumination; as such, it does not add to or increase our knowledge, "but illuminates the mind and its object as the sun illuminates the visible universe."[11] The light of Calvinism "adorns, fructifies, and vitalizes" knowledge;[12] but it does not provide, as the light of the Quakers does, the central and governing inspiration of life.

## III  *The New World*

The tumultuous upheaval that characterized the ministry of Fox was not uncharacteristic of the century in which the New Philosophy, as John Donne lamented, "Calls all things into doubt." In the year George Fox suffered his first imprisonment, 1649, Charles I was executed.[13] The early leaders of Quakerism were reared on the disorders of political and religious strife. Wherever one turned, there seemed to be a sect: the Familists, the Anabaptists, the Independents, the Sabbatarians, the Anti-

Sabbatarians, the Traskites, the Millenaries, the Etheringtonians, to name a few. And providing extremely fertile soil for the Quakers were the Ranters, the Seekers, and particularly the Baptists.[14]

In retrospect, we seem to feel there was a fury about the century; and, as we know from the sad history of the world, the reaction of established powers to dissent was often repression and persecution. That the Quakers survived at all in the welter of short-lived and often shattering enthusiasms of the age is somewhat remarkable. The personality of Fox, the redemptive vigor of his message calling all mankind into fellowship, and the conversion of men of great intellectual as well as spiritual stature such as Robert Barclay and William Penn to the side of Fox "in the darkest days of fierce persecution" account in large part for the survival of the Quakers.[15]

The Scottish theologian, Robert Barclay, took on the immense task of defining Quakerism and its view of man. In his great and classic defense of The Society of Friends, *An Apology for the True Christian Divinity* (1678), we find strong intellectual bearings which mark a decided change from the phrenetic messages of the first "Publishers of Truth." That there is a formulation of "doctrine" in itself suggests the beginnings of institutionalism. The church is now of the world with bickering as well as major problems attendant upon its establishment.

I find particularly interesting and significant Barclay's distinction between the inner light and reason. Barclay insisted on the subordination of reason to the divine light; but he affirmed that "we look upon reason as fit to order and rule man in things natural. For as God gave two great lights to rule the outward world, the sun and the moon, the greater light to rule the day, and the lesser light to rule the night; so hath he given man the light of his Son, a spiritual divine light, to rule him in things spiritual, and the light of reason to rule him in things natural."[16] This distinction between the inner light and reason achieved for Quakerism, I believe, what the triumph of nominalism over realism achieved for science toward the end of the Middle Ages—there was a spiritual world and a natural world. The Quaker could follow his own bent in the natural world without incurring a too-heavy burden of spiritual liability. This dualism had the effect of helping to bring the Quaker into accord with the empirical temper of the Age of Reason.

If we think of the first phase of Quakerism in the seventeenth century as one of prophetic and missionary zeal, and of the second phase as the establishment of the church and general consolidation of gains, then the third phase which begins in the last decade of the seventeenth century—Barclay and Fox died in 1690 and 1691—may perhaps be best summarized by John Woolman's view that Quakerism was undergoing a trial "by favor and prosperity." This trial is dramatically evident in "the holy experiment" of William Penn.

Frederick Tolles, indulging "in a brief flight of the historical fancy," wonders in a not quite half-serious mood whether George Fox atop Pendle Hill "facing westward toward the open ocean . . . could have foreseen another harvest of souls, farther in the future, in fields remote from Northern England, but just as dramatic, just as fateful, and, in the end, vastly more extensive."[17] Tolles writes that "no less than sixty men and women carried the Quaker message to the New World" between 1655 and 1662.[18] In 1671, Fox landed in Barbados and traveled extensively throughout the New World. Shortly after, the Quaker colonizing venture began. West Jersey was purchased, then East Jersey; and, in 1681, Charles II, in debt to Admiral Penn, paid it off by granting to the Admiral's son, William, the charter which made him Lord Proprietor of a vast province. In what was to become Pennsylvania, William Penn put into effect his plans for an ideal commonwealth.

The first Quaker colonists, as Tolles points out in his study of early Quaker merchants in Philadelphia, "carried with them" to Pennsylvania "sober words of advice and caution from George Fox . . . 'My friends, that are gone and are going over to plant, and make outward plantations in America, keep your own plantations in your hearts, with the spirit and power of God, that your own vines and lillies be not hurt.' "[19] Tolles characterizes the social history of Philadelphia Quakerism as "a record of two plantations." That the inner plantation, "the delicate plants of the inner life," did not flourish well "amid the unexampled flourishing of the outward plantation" is made abundantly clear by Samuel Fothergill, a great Quaker minister:

Their fathers came into the country, and bought large tracts of land for a trifle; their sons found large estates come into their possession, and a profession of religion which was partly national, which descended like a patrimony from their fathers, and cost as little. They settled in ease and affluence, and whilst they made the barren wilderness as a faithful field, suffered the plantation of God to be as a field uncultivated, and a desert. . . . A people who had thus beat their swords into plough-shares, with the bent of their spirits to this world, could not instruct their offspring in those statutes they had themselves forgotten.[20]

The Puritan values of worldly success as a sign of God's grace had permeated and formed in large part the commercial ethic of Quakerism as well as of Protestantism. The following advice given by William Penn to his children contains the phrase Benjamin Franklin was to make famous, "The Way to Wealth":

Diligence is [a] Virtue useful and laudable among Men: It is a discreet and understanding Application of one's Self to Business; and avoids the Extreams of Idleness and Drudgery. It gives great Advantages to Men: It loses no Time, it conquers Difficulties, recovers Disappointments. . . . Solomon praises Diligence very highly, First, it is the Way to Wealth: *The diligent hand makes Rich.* . . . Secondly, it prefers Men . . . *Seest thou a Man diligent in his Business he shall stand before Kings.* Thirdly, *it preserves an Estate.* . . .

*Frugality* is a Virtue too, and not of little Use in Life, the better Way to be Rich, for it has less Toil and Temptation. It is proverbial, *A Penny sav'd is a Penny got.* . . .

Trust no Man with the main Chance, and avoid to be trusted.[21]

This advice, sounding very much like Poor Richard's or Father Abraham's compendium of prudential virtues for Americans, suggests that the Quaker culture had become bourgeois by making a virtue of wealth. Therefore, when John Woolman was born in 1720 in West Jersey, within the influence of Penn's "holy experiment," the Quakers were a powerful and prosperous people who, intent on the "way to wealth," had strayed considerably from the way to God. Their debasement was most apparent in the fact that many of them bought, sold, and owned slaves.

We shall see that in 1755, under the strains of the French and

Indian Wars, the Quakers dominating the Pennsylvania Assembly and Quakers generally were forced by historical events to decide whether they were to continue to sacrifice the "inner plantation" for the cultivation of the "outward plantation." And John Woolman was to play a leading role during these years to help decide the outcome. Specifically, he sought to abolish slavery; to achieve equitable treatment of Indians; to vitalize Quaker pacifism; to return Friends to the promptings of the light within; and, finally, to free the spirit of man from material bondage. In John Woolman's movement of liberation, which persuaded Quakers to respond to the dictates of their own conscience, "he set the Friends as the cornerstone," as Edwin Cady suggests, "of the American libertarian conscience."[22]

## CHAPTER 2

# "A Consent and Good Will to Being"

**P**URCHASING TWO HUNDRED ACRES of land in the Delaware Valley before sailing from England, John Woolman's grandfather, also John, came to West Jersey two years after its incorporation in *The Concessions and Agreements Charter*. This document, drawn in 1766 under the influence of William Penn, is regarded generally by historians as a significant contribution to the development of constitutional democracy. The intent and good will of the proprietors of this document is evident in the statement that: "Thus we lay a foundation for after ages to understand their liberty as men and Christians, that they may not be brought into bondage but by their own consent; for we put the power in the people. No person [is] to be called in question or molested for his conscience or for worshipping according to his conscience."[1]

## I *The Plantation*

Under the provisions of this charter, trial by jury, voting by ballot, and representative government were established. Imprisonment for debt was abolished and so were religious qualifications for office. Because the Society of Friends into which Woolman was born was not a harried and persecuted minority, he, therefore, was not to be confronted with the dangers of a kind of cramping sectarian orthodoxy which persecution often tends to enforce. He was not to feel victimized by life because of his uniqueness or at odds with it, as the case might have been had he been born a Quaker in East Windsor, Connecticut, the birthplace of Jonathan Edwards. The Puritans' persecution of the Quakers in New England was as nasty as that practiced by their English counterparts.

Indeed, geography itself seems to have been more "liberalizing" or "tolerant" in West Jersey than in East Windsor. Our general image of early New England of an austere people as severe as their climate and as stony as their soil is not altogether false. The middle colonies provide a pleasant contrast. There we tend to think of a more temperate climate and of a more genial land that produced a people more amply generous in manners and taste as well as in kinds of religious belief. The Woolman plantation, long and narrow, fronted on the lovely Rancocas stream; for Penn and his fellow proprietaries had taken care to provide shorelines to as many plantations as possible. The stream, largely navigable, formed a juncture with the Delaware River six miles or so northwest of the Woolman homestead. Clearly, the days of the boy John were spent amid scenes of great beauty in which the rich variety of nature's colors did much to offset the plain severity of Quaker dress.

Woolman often uses paternity as a natural and endearing image of God: the Heavenly Father, the Father of Mercies, the Father of Lights.[2] He tells us that his father, Samuel, imparted to him "the true principles of virtue." Samuel Woolman was a man of affairs active in the business, social, and political life of the community. His wife, Elizabeth Burr, shared her husband's hopes and concerns; and she bore him a large family—John was the fourth child and eldest son among thirteen children—with tenderness of spirit and obviously with an admirable degree of perseverance. The plantation prospered.

Although Amelia Gummere characterized the Friends among whom John Woolman lived as "perhaps the most conservative community in the whole of Quakerism,"[3] a Quaker boy still had the freedom of sunny days on a river bank where he could step aside from his companions and read, think, and dream—as John Woolman often did. When he was thirty-six years old, he looked back to the boy who, by the shores of Rancocas, was reading in Revelation; "' He showed me a Pure River of Water of Life, clear as Crystal, proceeding out of the Throne of God and of the Lamb'&c. and in the reading of it, my mind was drawn to seek after that pure Habitation, which I then believed God had prepared for his servants. The place where I sat, and the sweetness that attended my mind, remain fresh in my memory" (151). It was as if the waters of the Rancocas, mingling with the memories of his boyhood, became the Water of Life itself. In the visionary richness of his imagination, he often made no distinction between nature and scripture, the reality and the image, the literal and the metaphorical, perhaps because in his most inspired moments he saw none. Even his dreams seem to coalesce with his waking moments as if there were no distinctions to be made between sleep and consciousness. Woolman relates a dream he had when nine years old:

> I saw the Moon rise near the West, & run a regular course Eastward, so swift that in about a quarter of an hour, she reached our Meridian, when there descended from her a small Cloud on a Direct Line to the Earth, which lighted on a pleasant Green about twenty yards from the Door of my Father's House (in which I thought I stood) and was immediately turned into a Beautiful green Tree. The Moon appeared to run on with Equal swiftness, and soon set in the East, at which time the Sun arose at the place where it comonly doth in the Sumer, and Shineing with full Radiance in a Serene air, it appeared as pleasant a morning as ever I saw.
>
> All this time I stood still in the door, in an Awfull frame of mind, and I observed that as heat increased by the Riseing Sun, it wrought so powerfully on the little green Tree, that the leaves gradually withered, and before Noon it appear'd dry & dead. Then there appeared a Being, Small of Size, moving Swift from the North Southward, called a "Sun Worm."
>
> Though I was A Child, this dream was instructive to me. (152)

Woolman's commentators have been puzzled as to how the dream was "instructive" to him. Perhaps Professor Edwin Cady is right, that "it would be presumptuous to pretend to interpret it now."[4] Amelia Gummere feels that there is no moral in it, hardly even an end, for "it terminates most abruptly."[5] Janet Whitney has suggested that John Woolman is the Being Small of Size, but "the definition of the words 'sun-worm' remain mysterious."[6]

Without attempting to interpret the dream, I think it can be related to the twenty-second chapter of Revelation which had inspired Woolman two years earlier on the shores of the Rancocas "to seek after that pure Habitation." In contrast to the revelation of hope and life that we find in the twenty-second chapter—to the images of the river of life and the fruit-bearing tree of life whose leaves "were for the healing of nations," where "there is no more night," where "they [the servants of God] need no light of ramp, neither light of sun, for the Lord God shall give them light: and they shall reign forever and ever"—is the satanic image of the worm and involution of light into heat. Woolman may have unconsciously associated his Sun Worm with the blazing star in Revelation, the star Wormwood, which, falling from the heavens, turns to bitterness one third of the waters of the earth. The brightness of the sky is thereby diminished, and those who drink of the waters will die.

Woolman thus developed early a profound sense of the provisional nature of our world. As a boy, his most poignant experience of the temporality of life was one in which he did the victimizing. On his way to a neighbor's house, he saw a robin "sitting on her nest":

> and as I came near she went off, but having young ones, flew about, and with many cries expressed her Concern for them. I stood and threw stones at her, till one striking her, she fell down dead. At first I was pleas'd with the Exploit, but after a few minutes was seized with Horror, as haveing in a sportive way kild an Innocent Creature while she was carefull for her young. I beheld her lying dead, & thought those young ones for which she was so carefull must now perish for want of their dam to nourish them; and after some painfull considerations on the subject, I climbed up the Tree, took all the young birds, and killed them supposing that better than to leave them to pine away and die miserably: and believ'd in this case, that scripture proverb was fulfilled, "The tender mercies of the wicked are Cruel." (152-53)

Woolman then continued on his way, but "for some hours could think of little else but the Cruelties I had committed, and was much troubled. . . ." And then Woolman writes: "Thus He whose tender Mercies are over all his works, hath placed that in the Human mind which incites to exercise goodness towards every liveing creature." To the degree that he recognized his Cruelties, to that degree he had become aware of the principle that had been "placed" in his mind by God. So it is that conscience matures.

Plantation life through gladness and pain was an awakening of Woolman's affections for all life. His was a firsthand experience

with nature, but his was also an experience in economic realities
—planting, growing, consuming, and trading. John's father was
also a weaver, for West Jersey plantations carried on the skilled
specializations of craft. The young John Woolman was nurtured,
therefore, by a self-sufficient agrarianism that was to inform much
of his later thinking about economics, politics, and social relationships.

## II  *Education, Vanity and Mirth*

The Quaker's realization of the light within often led him to
a fresh awakening of a divine regard for nature and all of creation. This consciousness is not very different from that kind of
spirit which Jonathan Edwards describes in *The Nature of True
Virtue* (1765) as "a consent and good will to Being in general."
The world and the spiritual world are unified by the kind of sensibility that says "Yes" to creation. Thus William Penn could
write, "It were happy if we studied Nature more in natural things
and acted according to Nature. These rules are few, plain and
most reasonable. Let us begin where she begins, go her pace, and
close always where she ends, and we cannot miss of being good
Naturalists."[7] Thoreau sounds the same note in *Walden* (1854)
with greater economy: "Let us live one day as deliberately as
nature."

Although we know little about the details of Woolman's schooling—he walked to a Quaker school about half a mile from his
home—it is not improbable that the emphasis was placed on an
education in things; in use; in the discipline and purification of
the self. There was no attempt in the country Quaker school to
inspire the intellectual life. Rudimentary education was sufficient
for the rustic Quaker: Why engender thoughts of a college or
university learning when the divine light was illumination
enough? Not even the ministry required special theological training. And we must remember that a practical education was essential for the variety of roles that a man was called upon to play in
colonial frontier life. Woolman himself was a farmer, a businessman, a shopkeeper, a teacher, a surveyor, a minister, a tailor, a
leech, and a legal adviser.

Perhaps the strongest influence on Woolman's schooling was
the home. "Through the care of my Parents," Woolman wrote, "I

was taught to Read near as soon as I was capable of it" (151). Reading was encouraged by the frequent practice on First Days, after meetings, when his parents "put us to read in the Holy Scriptures, or some religious books, one after another, the rest sitting by without much conversation, which I since often thought was a good practice" (151-52). Reading was further stimulated by Samuel Woolman's good library. We know also that, "having had schooling pretty well for a planter," John Woolman "used to improve Winter evenings, and other leisure times" (157).

And we must also remember that the country schooling of Woolman was quite different from that of the children of wealthy Quaker merchants in Philadelphia. These aristocrats were seeking to "improve" their children, to "cultivate" them by sending them abroad to study "the best" of European civilization. But they found some of their returning children spoiled by the Grand Tour, for "the richness of European life and society overcame the inherited concern for plainness, and they returned from their travels glittering young dandies laden with spoils picked up from Florentine art dealers, London haberdashers, and Parisian perfumers and jewelers."[8] Woolman's parents had no such worldly ambition for John; for he was educated in the virtues of plain speech, plain dress, plain food, a plain mode of life. The demarcation was already present, therefore, between those Quaker youths who were learning to live like aristocrats or at the least like bourgeoisie, and those few, rare spirits like Woolman who were learning the discipline that would lead ultimately to a meaningful, manly asceticism.

At the age of sixteen, Woolman began to associate with what he calls "wanton company." The biographer must take seriously Woolman's words—"and though I was preserved from profane language or Scandalous conduct, Still I perceived a plant in me which produced much wild grapes" (153)—but the critic must remember how conventional the "wild grapes" stage and the confessional are in the life and writings of mystics. For a period of five years Woolman's soul was in anguish and his tears copious. He fell ill, and in his illness he was seized with "darkness, horror, and amazement." He thought his recovery uncertain, and he repented of his ways. He made brave resolutions and professions of humility only to fall again. And what was the nature of his fall? He tells us: "I was not so hardy as to commit things scandalous, but to exceed in Vanity and promote myrth, was my chief study" (155).

The "wicked ways" of youth, the illness, the presence of death, the sense of God's closeness, repentance, recovery, and new-found resolution—often we find these stages in the spiritual records of divines and saints. We find them, for example, in Jonathan Edwards' *Personal Narrative* (1765); but surely neither Woolman nor Edwards was wicked—at least not as St. Augustine was wicked, for he had indeed walked the streets of Babylon. Woolman's agony, however, reflects his extreme sensitivity to the powers of light and darkness, as well as the intensity with which he sought to bring his will into accord with the "leadings" of the inner light.

Alternating between despair that ever he had been born and visions of the grace of creation, between illness and health, between irresolution and resolution, and between rebellion and contrition, Woolman emerged from this period with a new wonderment, a new sense of love "not only towards all men," as he movingly writes, "but allso toward the Brute Creatures. That as the mind was moved by an inward principle to love God as an invisible, Incomprehensible Being, by the same principle it was moved to love him in all his manifestations in the Visible world. That as by his breath the flame of life was kindled in all Animal and Sensible creatures, to say we Love God as unseen, and at the same time Exercise cruelty toward the least creature moving by his life, or by life derived from Him, was a Contradiction in itself" (156-57). Woolman had come to the new-found joy of his own discovered identity, of "this white stone and new name" which can be known only by those whose inward life have felt the beautiful presence of God. The discovered identity of the divine self is a kind of resurrection.

## III  *The Beginnings of His Ministry*

In 1740-41, John Woolman decided to leave the plantation; and, having received his father's permission, he went to the village of Mount Holly, about five miles from his home, to work as a clerk and bookeeper in the bakery and retail shop of a prosperous businessman. It is probable that his decision to become a townsman was in part influenced by the life of hard physical labor on a plantation and by the fact that John, if not a frail boy, did not seem to be robust: "In my youth I was used to hard Labour, and though I was midling healthy, yet my Nature was not fited to endure so much as many others..." (244). Perhaps, too, despite his fears of the temptations that were waiting for him in this more public world, the private life of the plantation had done all it could for him.

During the years 1740-41, the hints of a public ministry of some kind were surely prompting him. Having arrived at some tentative understanding of the meanings of his early life, Woolman had turned from the agonizing struggle of self-purification to the world outside the self. He was coming to an awareness of the "just sense of the conditions of others," and he had given his first utterance at meeting: "I went to meetings in an awfull frame of mind, and endeavoured to be inwardly acquainted with the language of the True Shepherd, and one day ... being under a Strong Exercise of Spirit, I stood up, and said some words in a meeting, but not keeping close to the Divine Opening, I said more than was required of me & being soon sencible of my error, I was afflicted in mind some weeks, without any light or comfort, even to that degree that I could take satisfaction in nothing" (159). Two years later his ministry was recognized and recorded, and Woolman felt "renewed engagements that in all things I might act on an inward principle of Virtue."

The "inward principle of virtue" was soon to be tested on two separate occasions. The first test marks the beginning of Woolman's public ministry and has to do with his visit to a rowdy tavern where frequent disturbances were troubling the community. "And I believed it was a duty laid on me to go and speak to the master of that house," Woolman writes, although the Quaker elders were aware of what was going on and had done nothing. It was during the Christmas season, one not celebrated by Friends because they believed Christ to be born anew in the soul every day:

> The Exercise was heavy, and as I was Reading what the Almighty Said to Ezekiel, respecting his duty as a watchman, the matter was set home more clearly, and then with prayer and tears, I besought the Lord for his Assistance, who in loving

kindness gave me a Resigned heart. Then at a sutable Oportunity, I went to the publick house, and Seeing the man amongst a company, I went to him and told him I wanted to speak with him, so we went aside, and there in the Fear and dread of the Almighty I Exprest to him what rested on my mind, which he took kindly, and afterward showed more regard to me than before. In a few years after he died, midle-aged, and I often thought that had I neglected my duty in that case, it would have given me great trouble and I was humbly thankfull to my Gracious Father, who had supported me therein. (161)

In observing the caution and gentle spirit in which this courageous deed was tendered, we realize how extraordinarily tactful Woolman must have been in the act of friendly persuasion. It appears that Woolman's chief concern was not with the disorder in the tavern but with the well-being of the tavern-keeper.

Shortly thereafter, a second occasion arose to test "the inward principle of virtue," and Woolman was forced into a momentary compromise:

My Employer having a Negro woman sold her, and directed me to write a bill of sale, the man being waiting who had bought her. The thing was Sudden, and though the thoughts of writing an Instrument of Slavery for one of my fellow creatures felt uneasie, yet I remembered I was hired by the year; that it was my master who directed me to do it, and that it was an Elderly man, a member of our society who bought her, so through weakness I gave way, and wrote it, but at the Executing it I was so Afflicted in my mind, that I said before my Master and the friend, that I believed Slavekeeping to be a practice inconsistent with the Christian Religion: this in some degree abated my uneasiness, yet as often I reflected seriously upon it I thought I should have been clearer, if I had desired to be Excused from it, as a thing against my conscience, for such it was. And some time after this a young man of our Society, spake to me to write an instrument of Slavery, he having lately taken a Negro into his house. I told him I was not easie to write it, for though many people kept slaves in our society as in others, I still believed the practice was not right, and desired to be excused from doing the writing. I spoke to him in good will, and he told me, that keeping slaves was not altogether agreable to his mind, but that

the slave being a gift made to his wife, he had accepted of
her. . . . (161-62)

This beginning of Woolman's active concern with slavery led
to his interest in the general welfare and education of slaves
and to a fully dedicated and active abolitionism.

## IV *Stability and Movement*

In 1743, Woolman set up shop for himself as a tailor and
retailer; but his choice of occupation had been made with difficulty. He had declined several excellent business offers. His
intelligence, his honesty, his industriousness, his remarkable per-
suasiveness with people—these traits presaged worldly success.
One line alone in the *Journal* suggests the conflict in his search
for a vocation; and, because the line is alone, it has pathos: "I
felt at times a disposition that would have sought for something
greater" (165).

As a businessman, he was industrious, keeping careful, diligent
accounts of every transaction. His concern for the poor who
were forced to buy on credit can be observed in his practice of
advising them in the purchase of "useful & not costly" goods.
He came to believe that, if one were honest, one traded only
in those things which were necessary and useful to people;
for the causes of evil in the economic system were traceable to
luxury and superfluity. His active concern for an understanding
of the economic conditions of his community is reflected in his
request to the constable for statistics on suits against debtors:
"Served 277 Warrants, 103 Summonses, and 17 Executions. As
to Writs served by the Sheriff, I got no account of them" (184).
Woolman himself once took a debtor to court, but this is the
only instance in which he did. He refers to the debtor as "an
Idle Man," and the debtor must have been.

Although Woolman was a strict collector of bills, Janet
Whitney reminds us there were many ways he exacted payment.
For example, Woolman would accept "produce or labour in
place of cash," and he practiced "the utmost patience and consideration where people were in difficulty. The produce or
labour was set down in the accounts with a money value attached, as, 'By work in my Meadow 2 shillings, By Henry

Choping wood at Door one shilling six pence, by weeving nineteen shillings one penny,' and so the account was gradually balanced to mutual satisfaction."⁹ It is probable that some trading in his early years on the plantation was in the form of barter; and he always was to think of labor and produce, rather than of money and gold, as the measure of a nation's wealth.

In 1749, Woolman, then a property owner as well as a successful tailor and shopkeeper, thought it was time "to settle," as he tells us; and he married "a well enclined damsel, Sarah Ellis." Their first child, Mary, was born in 1750. In 1754, Woolman's only other child, William, died three months after birth. In the *Journal*, there is no mention of the birth of either child or of the death of William; and his marriage was noted only as an afterthought in the final folio.¹⁰ We do not know, therefore, much about his marriage other than it seems to have been characterized by religious stability and conjugal affection.

The absence of detail about Sarah and Mary in the *Journal* may be accounted for by the fact that, in spite of his avowed desires for a simple home life of simple necessities, Woolman's great life was his apostolic life; and it does not seem unfit that he died on a foreign shore three thousand miles away from wife and daughter and Mount Holly. We must keep in mind that Quakerism in its early days owed much of its progress to the traveling ministry. In Woolman's day, the traveling ministry was still a means of vitalization of far-flung Quaker groups, although it was not fired with the evangelical zeal that had characterized its earlier periods. Indeed, the concept of the church from its beginnings was that of "a family of prophets, spiritually armed for the conquest of the world."¹¹

Although Woolman was no man for riding hardily over rough terrain, hunting the deer and fishing the streams by which he was encamped, he made numerous journeys of varying duration and distance beginning in 1743. While often sapping the strength of the physical man, these travels seemed to enlarge continually and to make robust the spiritual man. In journeying away from the secure comfort of home and family, away from hoeing and grafting and the innoculation of apple trees, and in going forward to the outcasts, the lowly and the oppressed, John Woolman was responding with a fine and quiet recklessness to the ministry of fellowship and liberation that had begun on Pendle Hill.

CHAPTER *3*

# The Apostle, I

THERE IS SOMETHING almost Quixotic in the image of Woolman riding forth to do war on a whole social, economic, and moral order which sanctioned human slavery. His success, however, was remarkable and genuine. The spirit of his age "dreaming of things to come," as the historian G. M. Trevelyan wrote, "spoke a new word through him...."[1] Trevelyan called the abolition of slavery for which Woolman spent a laboring life, "the Anglo-Saxon Revolution." Amelia Mott Gummere may be entirely correct in saying that: "More than any other one man, Woolman aided the English speaking nations to throw off the disgrace of slavery; and although so late as 1800, there were still 12,442 slaves held in New Jersey, of these, thanks to the labours of John Woolman, almost none were held by Friends."[2] And Edwin Cady observes that "there was no fully formed Quaker position on the subject until John Woolman formed it a century after Fox had begun his work."[3] Woolman believed that friendly persuasion which urged the natural rights of freedom for all men was powerful enough to overthrow the evil. Like Emerson, Thoreau, and Whitman, Woolman insisted that the only progress that was true was that which came about through self-reform.

## I *First Preaching Trip*

Three months after his recognition in 1743 as a minister by the Burlington Quarterly Meeting of Ministers and Elders, John Woolman was asked by Abraham Farrington to accompany him on a two-week preaching trip through northern New Jersey and East Jersey. Farrington, a convert to Quakerism, was now one of its more widely traveled ministers; and Woolman probably learned a good deal from this man who was thirty years his senior and an experienced missionary. If the concept of the church was that of a "family of prophets," then Woolman on this trip was a silent prophet. The voice of this ministry was Farrington's for these weeks were a kind of apprenticeship.

Woolman, learning some "profitable lessons," did not tell us what they were. He is inclined to simple notations, "Had an Evening at a Tavern in Brunswick, a Town in which none of our society dwelt. The room was full, & the People quiet" (163). This brief notation does suggest, however, the silent drama that must have taken place of a reverence that knows no sect. Woolman also writes that many meetings were held where meetings usually were not held, where there were no Quakers, or where there were a few Quakers and a good many Presbyterians. If one thinks of the political alliance between Anglican and Presbyterian in neighboring Pennsylvania, an unnatural alliance that had been formed to offset the political power of the Quakers,[4] then one is surprised and even amused to find Quaker meetings attended "chiefly" by Presbyterians.

The visit to Perth Amboy, an international port, aggressively commercial and prosperous, a prosperity that was founded in part on the slave trade, may have provided the most "profitable lesson" of the trip. It was undoubtedly a memorable occasion for Woolman when he left the meeting held in the Court House at Perth Amboy, at which many members of the Assembly were present, to breathe the fresh sea air and to gaze upon humanity in chains in the open slave-market.

## II  *The First Journey South*

In 1746, Woolman felt "drawings" for a journey to the back settlements of Pennsylvania and Virginia; and he was accompanied by Isaac Andrews, a descendant of the famous and notorious Andros or Andrews family. Sir Edmund Andros, governor of New York and later of Massachusetts, was made immortal by Nathaniel Hawthorne who characterized him as a despot, which he was. "The administration of Sir Edmund Andros lacked scarcely a single characteristic of tyranny," Hawthorne wrote in "The Grey Champion." But Isaac's family on the maternal side was Quaker; and Mary Wright, his grandmother, had been whipped in the streets of Boston because of her defense of Quaker belief. Andrews wanted to extend the trip to include Maryland and Carolina as well as wider travels through Virginia. This larger plan was most fortunate because from it came the larger experience of Woolman which stimulated his writing in 1746 of a remarkable essay, *Some Considerations on the Keeping of Negroes, Part I.*

In the all too brief account in the *Journal* of the trip is the strikingly strong divergence between Woolman's views and those of other diarists of the back settlements. We may think of Sara Kemble Knight, her aristocratic bearing on the New England frontier; or, more particularly because Woolman deals with the general Southern frontiers he visited, we may recall William Byrd and his justly famous description of "lubberland" in 1728:

> Surely there is no place in the world where the inhabitants live with less Labour than in North Carolina. It approaches nearer to the description of Lubberland than any other, by the great felicity of the climate, the easiness of raising Provisions, and the slothfulness of the people. Indian corn is of so great increase, that a little pains will subsist a very large family with bread, and then they may have meat without any pains at all, by the help of the low grounds and the great variety of mast that grows on the high land. The men, for their parts, just like the Indians, impose all the work upon the poor women. . . . When the weather is mild, they stand leaning with both their arms upon the corn-field fence, and gravely consider whether they had best go and take a small heat at the hoe: but generally find reasons to put it off till another time. Thus they loiter away their lives, like Solomon's sluggard, with their arms across, and at the winding up of the year scarcely have bread to Eat. To speak the truth, tis a thorough aversion to labor that makes people file off to North Carolina, where plenty and a warm sun confirms them in their disposition to laziness for their whole lives.[5]

Byrd's heavy, yawning humor and aristocratic perch is that of a cosmopolite, a Londoner who fancies himself the heir of the Renaissance. In contrast, Woolman speaks as a man of compassion and understanding, as a colonial with the emotive democratic tone that we like to think of as American:

Thence we crossed the River Susquehannah, and had several meetings in a new settlement, called Red Lands, the oldest of which did not exceed ten years. It is the poorer sort of people that comonly begin to improve remote Deserts: with a small stock they have houses to build, Lands to clear and fence, Corn to raise, Clothes to provide, and Children to Educate. That Friends who visit such may well sympathize with them in their hardships in the wilderness. And though the best entertainment such can give, may seem coarse to some who are Used to Cities or old Settled places, it becomes the Disciples of Christ to be content with it. (165-66)

His reactions to the "entertainment" of the slaveowners, however, is quite different: "When I eat drank and lodged free-cost with people who live in Ease on the hard toyl of their slaves I felt uneasie," Woolman writes, "and as my mind was inward to the Lord, I found, from place to place, this uneasiness return upon me at times through the whole visit" (167). Nevertheless, he heaped no scorn upon the slaveowners but extended his sympathetic nature toward them as he did toward "the poorer sort of people"; for his way was not one of self-righteous indignation but of love. Woolman, however, was no sentimentalist luxuriating in his affections for mankind; instead, he returned from this trip very much involved with the liberty of mankind, a newborn abolitionist.

## III *The Second Journey South*

Woolman's second trip to the South occurred in the spring of 1757. He was to travel eleven hundred and fifty miles by horseback during a two-month period.[6] His brother, Uriah, who had business to transact in North Carolina, provided him with companionship for part of the trip. The certificate of travel granted Woolman by the Burlington Monthly and Quarterly Meetings was for a religious concern. A Quaker traveling with this certificate could not use it for business opportunity. Uriah obtained a certificate "sutable to the ocasion."

Determined to keep the trip as uncompromisingly pure in principle as he could, Woolman decided not to accept kindness or hospitality that was given as a "gain of oppression." He provided himself in advance with pieces of silver to pay the slaves for the lodgings offered him by their masters. When he left a household where he had been received and entertained, he would speak to the head of the family in private giving him silver and telling him to distribute it to the Negroes. In some households, he himself gave the silver to the Negroes. Woolman argued that he must be free of obligation to the slaveowners, for he had in mind the biblical injunction: "Thou shalt not receive any gift; for a gift blindeth the wise, and perverteth the words of the righteous."

Woolman knew that the Apostles had traveled without provision, but "their labor in the gospel was considered as a reward for their entertainment, and therefore not received as a gift." But Woolman viewed his situation as being quite different:

> The entertainment the disciples met with, was from such whose hearts God had opened to receive them, from a Love to them, and the Truth which they published: But we, considered as members of the same society, look upon it as a piece of Civility to receive each other in such visits, and Such reception, at times is partly in regard to reputation, and not from an inward Unity of heart and Spirit.
>
> Conduct is more convincing than language; and where people by their actions manifest that the Slave trade is not so disagreeable to their principles but that it may be encouraged, there is not a Sound uniting with some Friends who Visit them. (188-89)

Although this kind of testimony obviously did not make for the most pleasurable social relationships, Woolman reports "that way was made easier than I expected, and few, if any, manifested any resentment at the offer, and most of them, after some little talk, accepted of them" (189-90).

Throughout the journey Woolman suffered intensely because of what he saw and experienced. A man tormented and sorrowed, the cry arose within him time and again, "Oh Lord! I am a Stranger in the Earth, hide not thy face from me." Because of his emotional situation, we sense a tenseness unusual for Woolman—an uneasiness and a testiness that end a conversation rather than allow it to open to persuasive possibilities. For example, he met a colonel on the road "who appeared to be a thoughtfull man." In the course of conversation, Woolman commented upon

the general differences between those who labored for a livelihood and those who lived on the labor of others. When the
colonel answered by describing the slothful disposition of the
Negro, Woolman argued that, if the Negro were free and if he
could cultivate that which was his, he would then find "satisfaction." But, since he had nothing to expect from life except
slavery for him and succeeding generations, there was no reason
for him to be other than he was; moreover, liberty was "the
natural right of all men equally." In the colonel's response that
the Negroes were better off in America than in Africa because
they lived better here, we can feel Woolman's temper rising.
He ended the conversation abruptly with the reply: "There's
great odds in regard to us, on what principle we act." Woolman
quickly added, however, that on another occasion where this
argument was used—the white man must save the Negro from
his wretched condition in Africa—he answered that, if compassion were our motive, we would not have enslaved the
Negro as we have (190-91).

And of course Woolman had to listen to the tiresome "scriptural" argument we hear even today: Negroes are the offspring
of Cain, and the color of their skin is God's mark upon them.
Woolman had no difficulty in demolishing this argument. Fur-
thermore, he reminded his listeners of the prophetic injunction
"that the son shall not suffer for the iniquity of the father, but
everyone be answerable for his own sins." This saying was to
provide a chief "text" for Part II of *Consideration on the
Keeping of Negroes* (1762). The reason men in "the darkness
of their Imaginations" held the kind of arguments they did is
traceable to "the love of ease and gain." Woolman grasped the
obvious motive with simple clarity.

He describes in his *Journal* some of the horrors he witnessed
of the Negroes' condition. Husband and wife are often parted
"beselling them far asunder, which is common when estates
are sold by executors at vendue." He records that

> Many whose labour is heavy being follow'd by a man with a
> whip, hired for that purpose, have in comon little else allowed but
> Indian corn and salt, with a few potatoes; the potatoes they
> commonly raise by their labour on the first day of the week.
> The correction ensuing on their disobedience to overseers, or

Sloathfulness in business, is often verry severe, and sometimes desparate.

Men and women have many times scarce cloathes enough to hide their nakedness, and boys and girls, ten and twelve years old, are often stark naked amongst their master's children. ... These are a people by whose labour the other inhabitants are in a great measure supported and many of them in the Luxuries of Life. These are a people who have made no agreement to serve us, and have not forfeited their Liberty that we know of. These are souls for whom Christ died and for our conduct toward them, we must answer before that Almighty Being who is no respecter of persons. (194)

Woolman found the churches he visited to be in states of despairing decline. He moved amidst sorrow and lamentation warning, "From small beginnings in error great buildings by degrees are raised" (193). But there were things to be said and won on behalf of truth. At the Yearly Meeting of 1757, Western Branch, in Virginia, several Pennsylvania queries were under consideration. The question, "Are there any concerned in the importation of negroes, or in buying them after imported?" was modified to "Are there any concerned in the importation of negroes, or buying them to trade in?" The query finally admitted was, "Are any concerned in buying or vending goods unlawfully imported, or prize goods?" Speaking on this last question, Woolman tried to put some firmness into it by observing that Quaker principles opposed "purchasing any merchandise taken by the sword" and that there was no other way of taking Negroes (195). Woolman raised no further protest after having had his say, but the point was made; and the final query, however broad, was, after all, progress.

There were no smashing victories on this trip. There are none in problems of this kind, but Woolman's voice was heard, and seeds of light had been planted. Equally important, Woolman was gaining the authority of experience that would prepare him for a major role in the Philadelphia Yearly Meeting of 1758.

## IV  *Newport*

John Greenleaf Whittier regarded the Philadelphia Yearly Meeting in 1758 "as one of the most important religious convocations in the history of the Christian Church."[7] At this meeting a committee was formed, of which Woolman was a leading member, to prepare the way for the abolition of slavery among all Quaker slaveholders under the jurisdiction of the Philadelphia Yearly Meeting. Naturally the work of this Meeting could not stop in Philadelphia or in Pennsylvania; other Yearly Meetings had to face the same issues of the Philadelphia session.

Newport was one of the chief centers of the slavetrade, and Quaker ships carried rum to Africa and slaves to America. Woolman, traveling through New England in the spring of 1760, spent a weekend at Newport, continued his travels, and then returned to Newport in time for the New England Yearly Meeting. On his first day at the meeting, a slave ship had come into the harbor. The sense of the closeness of evil made Woolman shudder: "I understood that a large number of Slaves were imported from Africa & then on Sale by a member of our Society.... At this time I had a feeling of the condition of Habakkuk, as thus expresst: 'When I heard, my Belly trembled, my lips quivered, my appetite failed and I grew outwardly weak, and I trembled in myself that I might rest in the day of trouble'" (234). At Newport he experienced his "day of trouble."

The legislature was in session at this time, and Woolman hoped for an opportunity to speak briefly before the House of Assembly. However, the prorogation of the assembly was expected daily, and Woolman decided his duty was at the Yearly Meeting rather than at the assembly. He prepared a memorial to be read to the legislature, but unfortunately we do not have the text of this petition. The petition was first read at the Yearly Meeting in an attempt to garner support for it, but Woolman failed to win the endorsement of the meeting although he did get the signatures of many Friends. Woolman's commentators generally feel that this petition was, however, the stimulus for anti-slavery work in the legislature. Janet Whitney writes: "Fourteen years later an Act was passed by the Rhode Island Legislature which prohibited the importation of Negroes, spoke of the right of personal freedom and enacted that, although all citizens and residents retained legal ownership of such slaves as they had, all slaves entering the state from the outside would become automatically free men."[8]

Despite the disappointment Woolman felt over the failure of his petition to gain full support, he could not leave Newport without meeting with some of the leading slaveowners among the Quakers. Approaching two Newport Friends and advising them of his desire, they encouraged him to meet with the slaveholders. The conference took place in the house of "a noted elder." After a period of silence, of meditation, Woolman spoke. "And at length," he writes, "feeling my mind released from the burthen which I had been under, I took my leave of them, in a good degree of Satisfaction." The meeting was an evident success: several members expressed a "willingness" to free their slaves "after their decease" (237).

The reader of Woolman's *Journal* is well aware of the great strain of the Newport trip. Woolman was unable to sleep. He records one occasion—a discussion on lotteries—of his losing his temper; and in a letter to his wife he confessed, "I am not so hearty and healthy as I have been sometimes . . ." (68). Undoubtedly the coming of the slave ship into the harbor and the sale of the slaves gave his mission an urgency of almost unbearable weight. It was as if he had looked into the horror of the universe. And yet, after his final conference with Friends, he wrote, "It is good for thee to dwell deep, that thou mayest feel and understand the Spirits of people" (238).

## V  *The Walking Tours*

Woolman ended his account of his second Southern journey with the story of a Mennonite who, traveling on business, was near the house of an acquaintance. He thought of staying the night with him, but as he passed the fields owned by his friend and as he saw the conditions of the slaves, "he kindled a fire in the woods hard by, and lay there that night." Afterwards, the friend having heard of this, asked the Mennonite why he had not come to the house for lodgings. The Mennonite answered him, "Ever since I lodged at thy field, I've wanted an opportunity to speak with thee. The matter was, I intended to have come to thy house for Entertainment, but seeing thy Slaves at their work, and observing the manner of their dress, I had no liking to come to partake with thee." And the Mennonite added, after further admonishment, "As I lay by the fire that Night, I thought that as I was a man of some substance, thou would have received me freely, but if I had been as poor as one of thy Slaves,

& had no power to help myself, I should have received from thy hand no kinder Usage than they have" (203).

This spirit, and perhaps this particular testimony of conscience, influenced Woolman in 1765 to make three journeys into Maryland on foot. To walk was to embody an image, to make real and literalize a metaphor. In *The True Harmony of Mankind* (1770), Woolman writes: "Walking is a phrase frequently used in Scripture to represent our journey through life, and appears to comprehend the various affairs and transactions properly relating to our being in this world" (444). He thought the walking tours would serve three purposes: (1) give to him "a more lively feeling" of oppression; (2) testify to "lowliness" before the oppressors; and (3) avoid pleasures, keep him "out of the way of temptation to unprofitable converse" (271).

During the first journey, the weather was particularly hot and dry. He traveled at a fairly rapid pace, and there was much "hard labor in meetings." At the time, he experienced severe fatigue and general discouragement. Seeking compensatory laws, he believed the fatigue to have been God's support of him—a kindness because he had been desirous of getting through the journey too quickly. It was as if God had chastised him and the journey had become a form of penance. In the heat and the dryness, in the wearying movement through dust, he came indeed to "a more lively feeling" of the state of the oppressed; and he found himself under a "humbling dispensation." This walk down the eastern shore of Maryland became, therefore, a walk of renewal and confirmation. Indeed, his walking tours were a culmination of all his journeys, of all his efforts to get closer and closer to the conditions of slavery, to make the conditions of the slave his own condition.

In his walk down the eastern shore, he had a companion, John Sleeper. His second walking tour, soon after, was down the western shore of Maryland; but he had no companion on this trip. He calls it his "lonesome walk," and he speaks of "this lonely walk and state of abasement and humiliation." But his mind was at rest, was "gathered inward." Woolman, who had a most profound sense of revivication of the sufferings of Christ and the Apostles, tasted misery and death; and, although dismayed, his spirit was beautifully softened. Woolman becomes for us man humanized through exposure, through the stripping of all outward modes of fashion and authority. The walking tours were the final reduction of Woolman's needs and wants: he had come as close as he could to "abject, houseless poverty."

Several months later he made a final journey into Maryland, but this time he did take advantage of travel on water. The purpose of his visit was the Maryland Yearly Meeting. "It was a journey of much inward waiting," he writes. And of these journeys, what could Woolman take home as a reward? His biographer, Amelia Gummere, believes there is a strong connection between Woolman's visits and the fact that "the public records of that period in Maryland and its borders show a large number of resulting emancipations."9 But for Woolman the result was simply the hope and trust, not the knowledge, that he had touched the hearts of other men.

## VI   Some Considerations on the Keeping of Negroes

Woolman wrote Part I of *Some Considerations on the Keeping of Negroes* soon after his return from North Carolina in 1746. He showed the manuscript to his father who suggested revisions and who, as Woolman says, "appeared well satisfied that I found a concern on that account." Woolman relates that in the fall of 1750, when his father was dying, "he being so far spent that there was no expectation of his Recovery, but had the perfect use of his understanding, he asked me concerning the manuscript, whether I expected soon to offer it to the Overseers of the press: and after some conversation thereupon he said, 'I have all along been deeply Affected with the Opression of the poor Negroes; and now at last my concern for them is as great as ever'." (173). But not until 1753 or 1754 was the manuscript, after several revisions, given to the Overseers of the Press to be examined by them; and, after "small alterations," it was published.

Woolman introduces his essay with an important distinction between natural affection and love. By natural affection Woolman means the ties of nature such as the protective care that animals and humans have for their offspring. Although the emotion is an instinctive one, it operates on behalf of reason because it provides for an order that is necessary to the welfare of the species, as in the case of the family bond. It may seem to be productive of the good for one's immediate family, but the affections are also self-limiting and may, therefore, be "productive of Evil, by exciting Desires to promote *some* by Means prejudicial to *others*" (335). To Woolman, natural love is a bias, a prejudice in our favor; and it is rooted in custom and opinion which are in accord with man's natural inclinations.

Woolman speaks, therefore, of an injunction that commands us to love our neighbor; indeed, we are commanded to love our enemy: "That important Injunction of our Saviour, Matt. vi 33, with the Promise annexed, contains a short but comprehensive View of our Duty and Happiness: If then the Business of Mankind in this Life, is, to first seek another; if this cannot be done, but by attending to the Means; If a Summary of the Means is, *not to do that to another which, in like Circumstances, we would not have done unto us;* then these are Points of Moment, and worthy of our most serious Consideration" (336). Our inclinations may have been formed and may be supported by custom and opinion, "But as the Judgments of God are without partiality, by which the State of the Soul must be tried," Woolman writes, "it would be the highest Wisdom to forego Customs and popular Opinions, and try the Treasures of the Soul by the infallible Standard TRUTH" (334). The chief consideration of this essay is, therefore, the seeking of others in love. And to seek love is to surrender the self to Truth, to Wisdom, to God.

Woolman believed that "LOVE *necessarily operates according to the* agreeableness of things, on principles unalterable and in themselves perfect" (335). There is a correspondence between his thought and certain views of Jonathan Edwards; for Edwards, in discussing the nature of true virtue, viewed the intent, the reason or motive behind an action, as the moral determinant of it. There could be no true virtue in any action unless love were present, and love, in all of its richness, means good will and benevolence and "consent to Being." It operates "on principles unalterable and in themselves perfect." Of course, Edwards' mystique is informed by, and ultimately succumbs to, dogma. This factor makes a significant difference between Edwards and Woolman, and we must caution ourselves against easy interchanges of words, expressions, and ideas. Both men believed divinity charges us and inspires us to love others; and, in loving others, we are coming closer to God, to the ultimate Other.

Woolman's argument is at times almost "legalistic," but it is always tender and compassionate. His emphasis is on the theme of the stricken sojourner, a theme of grief and pain. His appeal is to our humanity and to the common lot of all our beginnings. He asks his reader to remember

> . . . that all Nations are of one Blood, Gen. iii.20, that in this World we are but Sojourners, that we are subject to the like Afflictions and Infirmities of Body, the like Disorders and Frailties in Mind, the like Temptations, the same Death, and the same Judgment, and that the Alwise Being is Judge and Lord over us all, it seems to raise an Idea of a general Brotherhood, and a Disposition easy to be touched with a Feeling of each others Afflictions: But when we forget these Things, and look chiefly at our outward Circumstances, in this and some Ages past, constantly retaining in our Minds the Distinction betwixt us and them, with respect to our Knowledge and Improvement in Things divine, natural and artificial, our Breasts being apt to be filled with fond Notions of Superiority, there is Danger of erring in our Conduct toward them. (337)

His emphasis on the poignant theme of the weary stranger is a common one in Woolman's writings. It humanizes the thought of his essay, and it touches us for all men have sometime in their beginnings come out of the wilderness. And if a people now have the joys, the favors of providence, as Woolman writes, "it behooves them carefully to inspect their Ways, and consider the purposes for which those Favours were bestowed lest, through Forgetfulness of God, and Misusing his Gifts, they incur his heavy Displeasure whose Judgments are just and equal, who exalteth and humbleth to the Dust as he seeth meet" (337). The inspection of ways is a matter of seeing things as they are, not as custom has fashioned us to see them. It is trying the soul by its own truth. And in seeing things as they are, we must also see them as they ought to be; in this way, men try the soul by its truth.

At the center of the essay, Woolman postulates: "If I purchase a man who hath never forefeited his Liberty, the natural Right of Freedom is in him." The question naturally follows, "And shall I keep him and his posterity in servitude and ignorance?" (341). There is a fine ring of John Locke in the phrase, "the natural right of freedom." Woolman accepted it as axiomatic, as did his Philadelphia neighbor and future publisher, Benjamin Franklin; for both men were very much thinkers of the Enlightenment.

But slavery exists despite the natural right to freedom; and men are responsible for it. There are admittedly all kinds of difficulties attendant upon overthrowing a system that is so firmly established economically and socially as to become a way of life; but we cannot remedy it, Woolman argues, by continuing the oppression. And at this point the argument takes a turn characteristic of Woolman: he pleads not for the salvation of the slave, but for the salvation of the slaveholder. The slaveholder is corrupting himself and his children because there are no lawful wants for which slaves may be kept. A man keeps slaves because of his slothfulness and greed of "some glaring Shows of Riches." And the inheritance the slaveowner passes on to his children is degeneration:

> It appears, by Experience, that where Children are educated in Fulness, Ease and Idleness, evil Habits are more prevalent than in common amongst such who are prudently employed in the necessary Affairs of Life: And if Children are not only educated in the Way of so Great Temptation, but have also the Opportunity of Lording it over their Fellow Creatures, and being Masters of Men in their Childhood, how can we hope otherwise than their tender Minds will be possessed with Thoughts too high for them? Which, by Continuance, gaining Strength, will prove like a slow Current, gradually separating them from or keeping Acquaintance with that Humility and Meekness in which alone lasting Happiness can be enjoyed. (342-43)

Woolman thus uses "the old arguments" against slavery in a way which "transforms" them. As Sydney James sums up, Woolman was able to "attach slaveholding to the root stock of all evil acts, self-will."[10]

In Woolman's essay, practical and useful concerns are spiritualized; and word and thought often spring, therefore, into an exalted movement: "If we do not consider these Things aright, but, through a stupid Indolence, conceive Views of Interest, separate from the general Good of the great Brotherhood, and, in Pursuance thereof, treat our Inferiors with Rigour, to increase our Wealth, and gain Riches for our Children, what then shall we do when God riseth up and when he visiteth, what shall we answer him? Did not he that made us, make them? and *Did not one fashion us in the womb?*" (344-45). The question is rhetorical, but the anguished cry is Job's.

Between 1756 and 1760, probably closer to 1760, Woolman wrote Part II of *Considerations on the Keeping of Negroes* (1762). He speaks of "a care I felt growing in me for some years" for the Negro that made for the writing of the essay. He published the work at his own expense, although the Overseers of the Press offered to pay for its printing and distribution. Woolman felt that the "stock is the contribution of the Members of our religious society in general," and among them were slaveowners who might well object to its publication at their expense. He also felt that, if people paid for the book rather than having it given to them as a "gift," they would be more apt to read it "with Attention." The essay was printed by Benjamin Franklin, and it was sold at cost.[11]

In Part I, Woolman had argued for the "freedom" of the children of the slaveowner. Much of Part II is concerned with a plea for the freedom from slavery of the children of slaves. The text is, *The son shall not bear the iniquity of the father.* Woolman's argument is chiefly historical and legalistic. Well documented, it relies strongly on Old Testament statutes; but it draws upon various accounts of the slave trade such as Michel Adanson's, William Bosman's, and Joseph Randall's.[12]

As in Part I, at the heart of Woolman's argument is the self-evident truth that "Liberty is the Right of Innocent Men." The essay is also a study in the effect of an environment of degradation upon a people. And it offers a brief insight into a semantic that warps thought, that identifies "black" with slavery and "white" with liberty: Would we permit a white child to be a slave? The argument is rich in its sources, moving in its rhetoric, firm in its principles. The closing paragraph, compassionate and broad in its point of view, prophetic of doom and of hope, summarizes the essay:

> *Negroes* are our Fellow Creatures, and their present Condition amongst us requires our serious Consideration. We know not the Time when those Scales in which Mountains are weighed, may turn. The Parent of Mankind is gracious; His Care is over his smallest Creatures; and a Multitude of men Escape not his

Notice. And though many of them are trodden down, and despised, yet he remembers them: He seeth their Affliction, and looketh upon the spreading, increasing Exaltation of the Oppressor. He turns the Channels of Power, humbles the most haughty people, and gives Deliverance to the Oppressed at such Periods as are consistent with his infinite Justice and Goodness. And wherever Gain is Preferred to Equity, and wrong Things publicly encouraged, to that Degree that Wickedness takes Root, and spreads wide amongst the Inhabitants of a Country, there is real Cause for Sorrow to all such whose Love to Mankind stands on a true Principle, and who wisely consider the End and Event of Things. (381)

Part of that "End and Event of Things" was the Civil War. Whether or not the deliverance was God's, the price was to be paid in blood and tears. "Close your ears to John Woolman one century," G. M. Treveylan wrote, "and you will get John Brown the next, with Grant to follow."[13]

CHAPTER *4*

# The Apostle, II

THE MISSIONARY ENDEAVORS of the Quakers among the Indians was in part inspired by George Fox who told American Friends to "go and discourse with some of the Heathen Kings, desiring them to gather their Council and People together, that you may declare God's Everlasting Truth, and his Everlasting Way of Life and Salvation to them, knowing that Christ is the promise of God to them, A Covenant of Light to the Gentiles."[1] For William Penn, the conversion of the Indians to Christian belief involved considerably more than evangelical discourse since the realities of the frontier inevitably brought together Quaker and Indian into practical economic, political, and social relationships. Penn himself played a particular and noble role in "the protection and care" of Indians; large sums of money raised for the tribes, protective trade restrictions (including the prevention, not always successful, of the sale of alcoholic liquors), and fair treaties characterized Penn's rule.

For example, the *Concessions and Agreements Charter* of West Jersey, which as we noted earlier was drawn under Penn's influence, contains the following clause: "It is agreed, when any land is to be taken up for settlement of towns, or otherways, before it be surveyed, the commissioners or the major part of them, are to appoint some persons to go to the chief of the natives concerned in that land, so intended to be taken up, to acquaint the natives of their intentions, and to give the natives what present they shall agree upon, for their good will or consent. . . ." As Francis Kelsey has pointed out, this clause "was a fitting prelude to the later policy of Friends" and "epitomizes the land policy of Friends in West Jersey."[2]

## I  *A Time of Crisis*

The Indian Policy begun by Penn—which, despite strain and tensions amid French and Indian Wars raging in other colonies fitfully and fiercely since 1689, had kept the peace and hopes of amicability and mutual adjustments alive—collapsed in 1755 when war came at last to the Pennsylvania frontier. The year before, Woolman, dream-haunted as a prophet, saw the air afire, and streams of red extending from the sky into the earth; and he saw "a green plain," and a great multitude of men in a military posture, "some of whom I knew." He saw them as they passed his house. They were moving westward, "some of them looking up at me, and they expressed themselves in a scoffing, taunting way, to which I made no reply. Soon after, an old Captain of Militia came to me, and I was told that these Men were assembled to improve in the discipline of war" (175-76). Woolman's fearful vision was all too true for, as we know, in 1755, General Braddock's army, marching on Fort Duquesne, was defeated; the soldiers were scattered; and the general was mortally wounded. The horror of the scene, one of Braddock's officers wrote, "will haunt me to the hour of my dissolution."[3] The Great War of the Empire, the final phase of the struggle for control of a continent, had in fact begun.

Pacifism constituted a basic principle in the Friends' religious ideal of love to all mankind. How could they support the war in view of their religious beliefs? If they refused support, would not this course be an act of disloyalty to their provincial government? The Quakers, as Benjamin Franklin saw them, were in an indefensible position. Franklin writes that his years in the Quaker-dominated Assembly

> . . . gave me frequent Opportunities of seeing the Embarassment given by them by their Principle against War, whenever application was made to them by Order of the Crown to grant Aids for military Purposes. They were unwilling to offend Government on the one hand, by a direct Refusal and their Friends the Body of Quakers on the other, by a Compliance contrary to their Principles. Hence a Variety of Evasions to avoid Complying, and Modes of disguising the Compliance when it became unavoidable. The common Mode at last was to grant money

under the Phrase of its being *for the King's Use,* and never to enquire how it was applied.[4]

Franklin then proceeds to tell how, "when Powder was wanting (I think it was for the Garrison at Louisburg)," the Assembly voted on a request from New England for funds—but voted the three thousand pounds "for the Purchasing of Bread, Flour, Wheat, or *other Grain.*" The "other grain" was gunpowder.[5]

The Quaker legislature, in refusing to take a firm stand on the issue of the war and in resorting to devices by which they could declare themselves peaceable while allocating funds for arms and men, reflected the kind of hedging and compromise with history that threatened to destroy basic principles of Quaker belief and culture. To support peace, the Quakers would have to surrender their power in the legislature: the crisis of the times had forced upon them a decision. In 1755, when the General Spring Meeting met in Philadelphia, Woolman drafted an epistle signed by fourteen Friends declaring "it to be our duty to cease from those national contests which are productive of misery and bloodshed." In contrast to the worldly kingdom, Woolman images a spiritual kingdom on earth, "For as the Truth is but one and many are made partakers of its spirit, so the world is but one and many are made partakers of the Spirit of it: & so many as do partake of it, so many will be straitened and perplexed with it. But they who are 'single to the Truth, waiting daily to feel the life and virtue of it in their hearts, these shall rejoice in the midst of Adversity'..." (178-79).

Since Woolman's Epistle was a call for self-reform and purification of the whole of the Society of Friends, not the legislators alone but all Friends who compromised with principle because of worldly ambitions were summoned to a reawakening of the basic principle upon which the Quaker faith rested—obedience to the leadings of the inner light. Woolman traced clearly the practical consequences of individual action. Should a Quaker, for example, pay the war tax that had been levied in December, 1755? Woolman writes in his *Journal:*

Some of our members who are Officers in Civil Government are in one case or other called upon in their respective Stations to Assist in things relative to the wars, Such being in doubt whether to act or crave to be excused from their Office, Seeing their Brethren united in the payment of a Tax to carry on the said wars, might think their case nearly like theirs, & so quench the tender movings of the Holy Spirit in their minds, and thus by small degrees there might be an approach toward that of Fighting, till we came so near it, as that the distinction would be little else but the name of a peaceible people. (207)

And in the "Epistle of Caution" of December, 1755, Woolman took an unequivocal stand on the issue of the tax: "And being painfully apprehensive that the large Sum granted by the late act of Assembly for the Kings use is principaly intended for purposes inconsistant with our peaceble Testimony, we therefore think that as we cannot be concerned in wars and fightings, so neither ought we to Contribute thereto by paying the Tax directed by the said Act, though suffering be the Consequence of our refusal; which we hope to be able to bear with patience" (209). The adoption of this Epistle, as Professor Cady points out, "split the leadership of the Society of Friends and of the Quaker culture wide open. It was the beginning of the end."[6] By the following year, the Quakers, almost as a body, had withdrawn from the provincial Assembly.

As Robert Davidson has observed in his study of "the holy experiment" in Pennsylvania, "Strong opposition had not unseated them [the Quakers] before—nor had the threat of war. But this conflict disturbed them in many ways, and the most effective disturbance had been the preaching and arguments of Woolman, Fothergill, and Pemberton. They pointed out the digression from their original faith in the 'Rock of Defense' and the subterfuges of political expediency which had cloaked their actions more and more of late."[7]

With the collapse of political power of the Quakers, "the holy experiment" of William Penn had indeed come to its final end. Perhaps the natural aftermath of moral self-examination helps explain the great efforts the Quakers were now prepared to make on behalf of the Indian. For example, in 1756, the "Pennsylvania Friends had formed the 'Friendly Association for Regaining and Preserving Peace with the Indians by Pacific Measures.' Its purpose was to restore good feeling with the neighboring tribes,"[8] and in this they had some success in arranging for a great Indian

conference at Easton to discuss peace; but the conference failed
to accomplish anything worthwhile.⁹

The following year, The New Jersey Association for Helping
the Indians was founded and did have a substantial measure of
success. This association—John Woolman was a charter member—
hoped to provide a two thousand acre tract "of the best land that
can be got nigh or adjoining the Barrens"; for the Indians had
bartered away all their lands in New Jersey. In 1758, the Association's plans were "incorporated in the public policy", and
three thousands acres were set aside for the Indian. This tract
was "probably the first Indian reservation, properly so-called,
within the bounds of the United States."¹⁰

## II  *Passive Obedience*

When orders came to conscript men for the relief of the
English at Fort Henry and when the military officers meeting at
Mount Holly chose a number of Quakers to fill their quota,
Woolman's consideration of the position of the military is, inter-
estingly, in spite of his pacifism, sympathetic. "Amongst the
Officers," he writes, "are men of understanding who have some
regard to Sincerity where they see it"; and "To put them to
trouble on account of Scruples is a painfull task" (211).

He, however, shows some impatience toward Quakers who
were insincere and simply intent on avoiding "a dangerous employment." Some Quaker youth left Mount Holly; some decided
to become soldiers; and some honest youths who "could not bear
Arms for Conscience Sake" reported to the Captain of the Militia
and told him so; moreover, they also refused to hire other men in
their places since an "exchange" would have been morally indefensible. Woolman's natural sympathies were for these young
men; but, in general, he was not proud of the response of Quaker
youth to the draft: too many youths had avoided the draft rather
than offer themselves as "testimonies" to peace.

Woolman's direct confrontation with the military occurred in
April, 1758, when an officer informed him that he was to billet
two soldiers for which he would be paid properly. Woolman was
taken by surprise: "The case being new and unexpected, I made
no answer suddenly, but sat a time, silent, my mind being inward." He lodged the one soldier who came to the house, stayed

two weeks, "and behaved himself civilly"; but, when the officer returned to pay for the lodging, Woolman refused the payment: "I told him I could not take pay for it, having admitted him into my house in a passive obedience to authority." Woolman's statement of position was met with the officer's acknowledgment that "he was much obliged to me," an expression that made Woolman uneasy: "And afterwards being near where he lived, I went to his house and told him on what grounds I refused pay for keeping the Souldier" (212-13).

Woolman's integrity in opposing the war and thereby coming into conflict with civil government suggests to us at once his kinship with Henry David Thoreau. Thoreau, who spent a night in jail for his refusal to pay taxes that were raised to help finance the Mexican War, celebrated his action in the essay "Civil Disobedience" (1848). Both men expressed the belief that the individual conscience, actively exercised, could provide an incalculable moral force in the political life of a country; and among the means of exerting that force was "passive obedience" for Woolman and "passive resistance" for Thoreau. The distinction between "obedience" and "resistance" suggests temperamental divergencies: Thoreau held a jocular, if not cavalier and even contemptuous, attitude toward government; Woolman believed any act of resistance to his government to be "dreadful," but "to do a thing contrary to my conscience appeared yet more dreadful" (205).

In those unhappy days, when all political alternatives to war seemed to fail and when Woolman often felt that he was standing alone, he turned to the past for support—to the inspiration of men like Thomas à Kempis and John Huss. In particular, he thought of Huss and his opposition to the Council of Constance, "which the historian reports to have consisted of some thousand persons." In vindication of his conduct, Huss expressed this principle which Woolman quotes: " 'This I most humbly require and desire of you all, even for his sake who is the God of us all, that I be not compelled to the thing which my conscience doth repugn or strive against.' " And again, in his answer to the Emperor, " 'I refuse nothing, most noble Emperor, whatever the council shall decree or determine upon me, only this thing I except, that I do not offend God and my conscience' " (204-5). This principle Thoreau promulgated successfully, but never has it been practiced with greater charity than by men like Thomas à Kempis, John Huss, and John Woolman.

## III *Wyalusing*

In June, 1763, Woolman set out for Wyalusing, Pennsylvania, a place two hundred miles from Philadelphia, to visit the Indians on the east branch of the Susquehanna River. Papunahung, the chief of the Wyalusings, was a remarkable man who had been converted by David Zeisberger, a Moravian missionary, to Christianity. Reginald Reynolds mentions how Papunahung

> had prevented a blood feud once, when an Indian had been murdered by a white man; how he had been attacked and dangerously wounded with a tomahawk by one of his own people, but refused to take revenge when the man was caught; how, at the risk of being massacred, he and his tribe had refused to join other Indians in a war against the English Colonists "even if the fighting Indians should make slaves, or, as they expressed it, Negroes of them."[11]

Papunahung was known for his honesty in transactions of public business—he always refused gifts. And with a strong degree of acerbity, he not only understood that he could be "made" a Negro, but also he "marvelled"—since his Christianity had made of him a pacifist—that, as he said, "Christians were such great warriors."[12]

That Papunahung had kept his tribe at peace in the midst of the frenzy of war undoubtedly claimed the sympathies of John Woolman who, as we know, through strenuous effort had helped keep the Quakers at peace. Perhaps Woolman felt the need for a gesture of acknowledgment that the Wyalusing and the Quaker were united in their refusal to participate in the war and perhaps he hoped thereby to strengthen their fellowship. Woolman's inspiration for this apostolic journey to Wyalusing reflects the deep tenderness of his spirit: "Love was the first motion, and then a Concern arose to Spend Some time with the Indians, that I might feel and understand their life, and the Spirit they live in, If happily I might receive some Instruction from them, or they may be in any degree helped forward by my following the

Leadings of Truth amongst them" (254). Clearly there was no hellfire or damnation in Woolman's preaching; and we can observe in him the kind of evangelism—if sects must be evangelical—that soften, temper, and render beauty to the religious mission of only a few men.

The night before he left on his journey, Woolman was awakened from sleep by a man who took him to the public house where some newly arrived Friends had information for him. The Indians had taken a fort and "had slain and scalped" some English near Pittsburgh "and in divers places." But Woolman believed he had to continue with the trip, although he was fearful that he might be prompted to undertake it at this time by his reputation as a man rather than by the "leadings" of truth. Besides the Indian guides, he was joined by a Friend, Benjamin Parvin. Woolman was reluctant to allow Parvin to accompany him; "for, as the Journey appeared perilous, I thought if he went chiefly to bear me Company, and we should be taken captive, my having been the means of drawing him into these difficulties would add to my own Affliction" (251).

Woolman writes that: "After I had given up to go the thoughts of the Journey were often attended with unusual Sadness..." (249). There is a reflectiveness and brooding seriousness in his account of his daring journey that quiet us and that present to us moral realities more forcefully than would the physical danger and the excitement: "And as it pleased the Lord to make way for my going at a Time when the Troubles of war were increasing, and when by reason of much wet weather Traveling was much more difficult than usual at that Season, I looked upon it as a more favourable Oportunity to season my mind, and bring me into a nearer Sympathy with them [the Indians]" (254).

Woolman, acutely sensitive to nature, suggests a correspondence between the natural scene and his inmost thoughts when he writes, "The Sun appearing we set forward, and as I rode over the barren Hills my meditations were on the Alterations of the Circumstances of the Natives of this land since the coming in of the English" (254-55). We see not only the barren hills, but the "alterations" of hills are conjoined with the "alterations" of circumstances, a movement imparting impulse and rhythm to his thought. The barren hills lead him to thoughts about the fertile and productive land the Indians once had and how they "for

small considerations sold their Inheritance so favourably Scitu-
ated and in other places been driven back by superior force"
(255). The unusual sadness was the reflective note of the pastoral
and the elegiac.

As incident leads to meditation, his thoughts, however familiar
to a reader of the *Journal,* take on greater significance; a new
life is breathed into them because of the experiences from which
they are formed. Woolman tells of how, near his tent, he sees
"on the sides of large Trees peeled for that purpose," scenes of
battles, of the going and coming of men in war, and of men dying
in battle, "this being a path heretofore used by warriors. And as I
walked about viewing those Indian histories, which were painted
mostly red but some with black, and thinking on the Innumerable
Afflictions which the proud, fierce Spirit produceth in the
world," Woolman imagines the warriors "traveling over Moun-
tains and Deserts"; and he knows their "Toyls and fatigues."

He reflects "on their miseries & Distresses when wounded far
from home by their Enemies, and of their bruises and great
weariness in Chaseing one another over the Rocks and Moun-
tains, and their restless, unquiet state of mind who live in this
Spirit, and of the hatred which mutually grows up in the mind
of the Children of those Nations Engaged in War with each
other." He faces with candor the generative consequences of their
afflictions and oppressions—hatred. And Woolman's immediate
response is characteristic—there "arose very fresh" in him "the
desire to cherish the Spirit of Love and peace amongst these
people" (253).

In thinking of the Indian, Woolman's sympathies are extended
to the straitened people on the frontier whose plight is caused
by their necessity to escape the wealthy "who often set high rents
on their land." And some of these frontiersmen settle land which
they did not buy from the Indians and which they often gained
by "that wicked practice of selling rum." Woolman himself had
"once some years ago retailed Rum, Sugar, and Molasses, the
fruits of the labour of slaves but then had not much concern
about them, save only that the Rum might be used in modera-
tion" (281).

Woolman's heart was indeed heavy; his concern, weighty. He
kept before his view the "favorable situation" of the English and

the degeneracies to which Negroes and Indians were subjected
by them. Like an Old Testament prophet, perhaps like Jeremiah,
Woolman writes, "And here Luxury and Covetousness, with the
numerous Opressions and other evils attending them, appeared
very Afflicting to me, and I felt in that which is Immutable that
the Seeds of great Calamity and desolation are Sown & growing
fast on this Continent" (256).

When Woolman and Parvin reached the Indian settlement at
Wyoming, Pennsylvania, no sooner had they settled their baggage
than they perceived an Indian with "a Tomahawk wrapped under
his matchcoat out of sight." Woolman went forward and ap-
proached him with open friendliness. This incident is particularly
interesting, for Woolman on his arrival had heard the news
brought by Indian runners that hostile Indians had taken an
English fort to the west, that they had killed its inhabitants, that
they were preparing for another assault on another fort, and
that the previous night two Indian warriors had come into
Wyalusing—Woolman's destination—"with two English Scalps,
and told the people that it was War with the English." In view
of this information, Woolman's response to the Indian with the
tomahawk is admirable; and we may be amused with the true-
ness of his courage when he writes, "Though his taking his
hatchet in his hand at the instant I drew near him, had a dis-
agreeable appearance, I believed he had no other intent than to
be in readiness in case any violence was offered to him" (257).

These new developments of increasing and immediate danger
naturally led Woolman to further self-examination as to his
motives for the trip: "In this great distress I grew jealous of
mySelf, lest the desire of Reputation, as a man firmly settled to
persevere through dangers; Or the fear of disgrace ariseing on
my returning without performing the visit might have some place
in me." Intent on strict obedience to the will of God, his problem
was one of determining which voice was God's and which his
own vain voice. Out of the conflict he gathered a renewed sense
of the purpose of his mission; the creature had been put to rest;
God "was pleased to give quietness" (257). Moreover, there were
to be no more outward alarms; in fact, there was, instead, help
from famous Indians like Job Chilaway and Jacob January who
joined Woolman and Parvin for awhile; and the first Indian they
met at Wyalusing was "a woman of modest countenance, with

a Babe." The threat of war seemed to disappear in the presence
of a mother and her child.

On the way to Wyalusing, Woolman and Parvin had been
overtaken by David Zeisberger and an Indian companion. The
Moravians had been the chief missionaries to the Wyalusings,
and Zeisberger's haste may have been due to fear that the Quakers were out to win converts for their sect. But there was to be
no race to Wyalusing, for Woolman would rival no one nor would
he compete for the saving of souls. But the Indians were worried
when Woolman arrived. They knew "that the Moravian and I
were of different Religious Societies, and as some of their people
had encouraged him to come & stay awhile with them were I
believe concerned that no jarring or discord might be in their
meetings." Woolman masterfully allayed all fears and established
a pleasant harmony by telling Zeisberger that he would hold no
meetings. He would simply attend the Moravian meetings, and
he might sometimes speak there "when love engaged me thereto"
(260).

Perhaps the climactic moment of the trip occurred on the
evening of June 18 at the Moravian meeting when Woolman was
moved to speak. After laboring for awhile with an interpreter,
he was so taken up by "the spirit of prayer" that he finished
speaking without an interpreter. When the meeting was over, he
observed Papunahung talking to one of the interpreters. What
had the Indians understood when they knew little or no English?
What divinity could be at work to make for understanding?
Woolman afterwards learned Papunahung had said "in substance"
to the interpreter: "I love to Feel where words come from" (260).

The sympathy Woolman must have established with the Indians is suggested by his own attitude toward them: "I thought
that the Affectionate care of a good man for his only Brother in
Affliction, does not exceed what I then felt for that people." The
paradox, of course, is that he came to the Indian, his brother;
but he was fearful of the Indian, his enemy: "I came to this place
through much trouble; & though through the Mercies of God, I
believed that if I died in the Journey it would be well with me,
yet the thoughts of falling into the hands of those Indian warriors, was in times of weakness afflicting to me" (261). Yet the
incident at Wyoming was the way of Woolman—of a man who
tried to follow without conditions the principles of the Sermon

on the Mount. With great courage he had walked toward the Indian who had the tomahawk; and he had extended a hand, open and in friendship. This act was one of grace.

## IV *The Apostle as Mystic*

We have seen that Woolman's apostolate—indeed, the expression and conditions of his life—was "moved" primarily by what he felt to be the "operations of divine love." In an age such as ours, we have witnessed the horrors of altruisms committed in the name of love:

> Love that listens where the good,
> The Virtuous, the men of faith,
> Proclaim the paradise on earth
> And murder starve and burn to make it.

Thus Archibald MacLeish in "Pole Star For This Year" speaks for the experience of our time. Words, therefore, such as "love" and "truth" and "spirit" are always in need of contextual definition. We have understood Woolman's "divine love" within the context of the Quaker faith which, as we have said, was founded upon the "leadings" of the inner light, a distinctive form of mysticism suggesting an intuitive mode of perception. A Quaker in the moment of his response to the inner light has, therefore, become a mystic. True, the moment cannot be sustained for most believers; but in Woolman the moments of inspiration were of a frequency and intensity that finally proved durable—mysticism was the essential quality of his mind.

There are various ways of defining the mystic—we might begin, say, with Heraclitus and with Plato—but this would prove tiresome for our purposes. Nor is it necessary for us to engage in philosophical and weighty matters that Woolman did not engage in, as to whether intuition and reason are mutually exclusive modes of cognition or whether evil is an illusion or whether time is an illusion. Such discussions at best tend toward the mechanical and the abstract, complicating that which is not complex: Woolman moved through the world a man of reason, a man of the Enlightenment whose voice, however different the accent, was contemporaneous with the voices of Voltaire, Rousseau, Paine, and Franklin. The supreme voice, the voice within, was divine reason; but divine reason was, after all, reasonableness. Woolman could turn to it for motion and direction. The inner voice or light was the foundation for his humanity because it was the voice or light of love rather than the narrow grating self-will of natural affection. Woolman uses the word "drawings" time and again— "Of late I found drawings in my mind to visit New England"— and by "drawings" he meant the leadings of the Holy Spirit within. And, because God led him, his experience is divinified.

There was in his mysticism an element of the ecstatic, the ecstatic paradoxically without rapture or frenzy. Woolman had at times the dreams and visions of the saint, the kind of thing that suggests John or Paul. For example, he writes in 1772, the year of his death, the following:

> In a time of Sickness with the plurisie, a little upward of two years and a half ago I was brought so Near the gates of death, that I forgot my name. Being then desirous to know who I was, I saw a mass of matter of a dull bloomy collour, between the South and the East, and was informed that this mass was human beings, in as great misery as they could be, & live, and that I was mixed in with them, & henceforth I might not consider myself as a distinct or Separate being. In this state I remained several hours. I then heard a soft, melodious voice, more pure and harmonious than any voice I had heard with my ears before, and I believed it was the voice of an angel who spake to the other angels. The words were *John Woolman is dead.* I soon remembered that I once was John Woolman, and being assured that I was alive in the body, I greatly wondered what that heavenly voice could mean. I believed beyond doubting that it was the voice of an holy Angel, but as yet it was a mystery to me. (308-9)

In his vision, he is carried "to the mines" where he finds an oppressed people who are "digging rich treasures for those called Christians." The oppressed blaspheme Christ, for the followers of Christ are oppressing them. In the morning, Woolman, not quite sure who he is, asks his wife and others at his bedside if they know who he is. The mystery is deep, and he must come to an understanding of it:

My tongue was often so dry that I could not speak till I had moved it about and gathered some moisture, and as I lay still for a time, at length I felt divine power prepare my mouth that I could speak, and then I said, "I am crucified with Christ, nevertheless I live yet not I, but Christ that liveth in me, and the life I now live in the flesh is by faith in the Son of God who loved me and gave himself for me." The Mystery was opened and I perceived there was Joy in heaven over a Sinner who had repented, and that that language, *John Woolman is dead,* meant no more than the death of my own will. (309)

This experience and the interpretation of it are characteristic of the mystical seeing and probing of Woolman. For nearly one year after this vision, he could not speak at meetings because he felt the misery of the slaves with an intensity for which he could find no words. Woolman was "shut up from speaking," but he was alive to his soulful ministry and in tears.

Or perhaps a more "classic" kind of illumination is the one which occurred in May, 1757. Woolman awoke to see a light in his chamber which he described most exactly as being

at the apparent distance of about five feet, about nine inches diameter, of a clear easie brightness, and near the center the most radient. As I lay still without any surprise looking upon it, words were spoken to my inward ear which filled my whole inward man: They were not the effect of thought, nor any conclusion in relation to the appearance, But as the language of the Holy One Spoken in my mind: the words were *Certain Evidence of Divine Truth,* and were again repeated exactly in the same maner, whereupon the light disappeared. (187)

Although we shall have occasion to return to this dream again in a later chapter, the point to be made now is that, in his belief in the Quaker creed, Woolman was a mystic as all Quakers are mystics. In his visions and his dreams, in his amazing sensitivity to the God Whose seed he believed was within him, in the attempts at purification which would lead to a dissolution of the self to realize the will of God, in the ways of reception to divinity, Woolman became "nonsectarian." He was, in the end, not a special kind of mystic, a Quaker—but a mystic.

Woolman's mysticism was not wholly untutored, for Walter Altman has made a good case for Woolman's wide readings in

mystical works and the influence these works had in providing
him with some insights into "the central truths" of mystical "tra-
ditions."[13] Frederick B. Tolles has published a ledger which
Woolman kept of books he had loaned to friends, and this ledger
suggests and lists some of the reading Woolman must have done
in writings of mystical persuasion.[14] Rufus Jones, commenting
upon Amelia Gummere's assertion of Fenélon's strong influence
on Woolman, refers to other influences, those, for example, of
Madame Guyon and Miguel de Molinos, the seventeenth-century
Spanish saint.[15] (Altman feels it is unlikely that Woolman read
Molinos, and that he read Fenélon, Altman believes, is supported
only by circumstantial evidence).[16] In general, Woolman's
thought was influenced by these and other writers who professed
a mysticism, a way of seeing that came late in Christianity, during
the Reformation, and expressed itself in Catholic as well as
Protestant theology. Perhaps the work most popular that reflects
this thought is Thomas à Kempis' *The Imitation of Christ,* and
the school of mysticism is Quietism:

> Of course Catholic quietism and Quaker quietism were not quite
> the same thing. We may say in general, however, that Quietism
> is a form of mysticism which starts with the assumption of the
> essential moral ruin and religious incapacity of human nature,
> which Paul calls "the flesh." It is something other than the
> selfishness and wilfulness of personal human desires set over
> against the will of God. It implies that all of the "human
> creature," as distinct from the divine manifestations in the form of
> supernatural "motions," "breathings" or inspiration, is wholly
> and unworthily other than the divine. Quietism believes, there-
> fore, that God can work within and through the human spirit
> only when the usual activities of the "creature" are "quiet"; that
> only in the "silence of all flesh" can God make himself heard;
> that only when all "creaturely activities" of reason, forethought,
> planning and organization are suspended can God work in and
> direct the soul through some invasion, a "breaking in" or
> "prevailing" of the Divine.[17]

Quietism was in part a reaction against the inflexible official-
dom of the Catholic Church in counter-Reformation movements.
The Jansenists at Port Royal are a good example of the Quietistic
reform movement within the Church. The Jansenists believed

that the individual, purified conscience was the voice of God in a direct communion with man. To them, that which is deliberated is not God's; for thought and the will must be put to rest before man becomes the instrument of God. *John Woolman is dead:* only under this condition is purity to be achieved. But Quietism does not mean mere passivity; for, as Rufus Jones cautions, we "must not make the mistake of supposing that Quietism means inaction and folded hands . . . It was not a question of action or non-action; it was a question of the right way to initiate action."[18]

Man is unable to affect anything spiritual in his unadorned humanity. There is the divine, and there is the human; but there is no meeting of the two except in the spirit that Woolman reflects when he writes, "There is a principle which is pure, placed in the human mind, which in different places and ages hath had different names; it is, however, pure and proceeds from God. It is deep and inward, confined to no forms of religion nor excluded from any, when the heart stands in perfect sincerity. In whomsoever this takes root and grows, they become brothers."[19]

Quietism had no paralyzing effect on Woolman. On the contrary, it taught him greater spiritual discernment. He sought purity, and he waited upon God; and, in the waiting, there came to him leadings; and the leadings took him to the Negro and the Indian. Quietism in its influence on Woolman did away with philosophical speculations and doctrinaire controversies. Paradoxically, "creaturely quiet" helped make Woolman a man of action, a practical mystic, and an armed prophet.

## CHAPTER 5

# Economy

W E HAVE discussed briefly Woolman's view that Quakerism in America was undergoing a trial by "favor and prosperity." Economic advancement, we said, was one of the strong motives for Quaker emigration, for the Quaker was not unlike the Puritan in his high regard for the ignoble ethic that the prosperous were God's chosen people. The Quaker, however, did not look upon the poor as people in disgrace with God while the Puritan generally tended to think of poverty as a sign of grace withheld. Despite the biblical admonition that it is easier for a camel to pass through the eye of a needle than it is for a rich man to enter Heaven, the Puritan managed to believe that the road to wealth was the way to heaven. The Quaker, finding himself caught between two conflicting ideas, all too often decided to compromise with his conscience and come to terms with the world. A rare spirit could find resolution by curtailing all outward business.

## I *"Right Livelihood"*

In 1756, while the large issues of war and peace were being argued in the Assembly, John Woolman, in a personal and intimate action, eloquently reinforced his plea for peace and self-reform within the society by freeing himself from "outward cumbers." Until this year, we recall, Woolman had been a tailor and shopkeeper: "I began with seling trimings for garments, and from thence proceeded to Sell cloaths and linens, and at length having got a considerable shop of goods, my trade increased every year, and the road to large business appeared open: but I felt a Stop in my mind" (182). The increase of business had become his "burthen." Principles could have no meaning unless they were acted upon: "I then lessened my outward business; and as I had opportunity told my customers of my intention that they might consider what shop to turn to: and so in a while, wholly laid down merchandize, following my trade as a Taylor, myself only, having no prentice" (183).

Although Woolman's renunciation of wealth was in sharp and bold contrast to the pursuit for riches of many of his Quaker contemporaries, his action had ample precedent—a stage of spiritual development not uncommon in Quaker history nor generally in the records of men of mystical persuasions. Aldous Huxley, in his introduction to an edition of the *Bhagavad Gita*, discusses the Gita teachings of "holy indifference to the fruits of action." Holy indifference must "be taught in conjunction" with what "is called 'right livelihood'." Huxley then speaks of Woolman as "a most enlightening example of the way in which a man may live in the world, while practicing perfect non-attachment and remaining acutely sensitive to the claims of 'right livelihood'."[1] Woolman was not aware of Oriental philosophy and theology; his way is suggestive, however, of the *Bhagavad Gita*—something that is not unusual in American literature.

It is noteworthy that the American Transcendentalists, Emerson, Thoreau, and the one-time Quaker, Whitman, were all aware in varying measure of Hindu scripture—were all examples of men concerned with the special qualities of "right livelihood." They shared Woolman's vision of life: that there is a unitive knowledge to be found where God or Brahma is realized, and men are to live in agreement with the insights gained by this realization. Emerson wrote in the back of his copy of Woolman's *Journal*, "I find more wonderful wisdom in these pages than in any other book written since the days of the Apostles. There is a true philosophy—a clear insight—a right estimate of things."[2] Woolman was grounded in the severe practicalities of the world, and yet he practiced an "aloofness" in which self-will was abolished and actions made pure.

By non-attachment, Huxley means, "a holy indifference to the fruits of action." Huxley quotes Albert Camus as saying, "He who refers every action to God . . . and has no aims save His glory, will find rest everywhere, even amidst the most violent commotion."[3] Woolman was a practical mystic, a mystic who referred every action to God; but he was engaged in the fierce activity of the world. He sought "right livelihood" as a fact of ultimate practicality.

Woolman's decision to lessen his outward business for fear of being ensnared by the superfluities and luxuries of prosperity is an instance of the principle of "right livelihood." This principle is extended further, for example, when Woolman, in 1770, believing "it is required of me to be resigned to go on a visit to some part of the West Indies," refused, after much travail of spirit, to go because he would not take passage on a ship engaged in the West Indies trade. Anything to do with profits of slave labor was an abomination that supported oppression. For a time he thought he might go in good conscience if he paid more than the low rates of common passage, for the low rates were possible because of the profits from slavery.

Sailing to England in 1772, in poor health—indeed, the year of his death—Woolman lodged in the steerage despite the pleading of friends that he take a cabin. He gives us the reason he would not; sensitivity to the claims of "right livelihood" for one's self is also sensitivity to the claims of "right livelihood" for others:

> I told the owner that on the outside of that part of the Ship where the cabbin was, I observed sundry sorts of Carved work and Imagery, and that in the Cabbin I observed some superfluity of workmanship of several sorts, and that according to the ways of mens reckoning, the Sum of money to be paid for a passage in that Appartment has some relation to the Expence, in furnishing the room to please the minds of such who give way to a conformity to this world; and that in this case, as in other cases, the moneys received from the passengers are calculated to answer every expense relating to their passage, and amongst the rest the expence of these superfluities. And in that case I felt A scruple with regard to paying my money to defray such expences. (290)

In England, Woolman refused to ride the stagecoaches and warned his friends not to send letters to him "on any common occasion" by post because of the brutal treatment of postboys, some of whom froze to death riding atop the coach in furious journeys through the winter nights. The claims of "right livelihood" also extended to brute creation, for Woolman was concerned about the horses. It was not uncommon for them "to be killed with hard driving, and that many others are driven till they grow blind." Woolman's words on the English stagecoach could have been a quotable prefix for Thoreau's chapter "Economy" in *Walden:* "So great is the hurry in the Spirit of this world, that in aiming to do business quick, and to gain wealth, the Creation at this day doth loudly groan!" (306).

Perhaps the best example we have of a personal, intimate code of "right livelihood" is Woolman's concern in later life over the wearing of undyed clothing. One of Woolman's fundamental principles of labor was that it should be "an agreeable employ." If men lived in "humility and plainness," then a reduction in certain kinds of demands for labor would take place. The ideal way of living is founded on a simplicity that insists on keeping "to that use of things which is agreeable to universal righteousness." The dyes of cloth were furnished by slave labor of the West Indies, the dyes were injurious to the cloth, and undyed cloth was cleaner.

In 1761, after a long illness and recuperation, Woolman felt he was undergoing a purgation and purification; and he decided to give up the wearing of dyed clothing. This decision was made not without supplication and tears, for Woolman feared that eccentricity of appearance could handicap the labor of his ministry. Although he did not look upon the wearing of undyed clothing as an evangelical mission, ten years after his decision he was still confirmed in it; and he commented upon it in the *Journal.* He had been traveling in England; the streets of the towns and villages were narrow, the weather wet, and the air "infected" with the scent of "dirtiness" and "filth": "And I being but weakly, have felt distress both in body and mind with that which is impure. In these journeys I have been where much cloath hath been dyed, and sundry times have walked over ground where much of their die stuffs have drained away. Here I have felt a longing in my mind, that people might come into Cleanness of spirit, Cleanness of person, Cleanness about their houses and Garments" (312).

Woolman then distinguishes between "delicacy" and "cleanliness." Delicacy hides, colors; but cleanliness is an expression of sincerity, of holiness of spirit. "And if the value of die stuffs, the expense of dieing, and the damage done to Cloath, were all added together and that expense applied to keep all sweet and clean, how much more cleanly would people be!" (312).

At times we may be struck by a straitened and strained if not moribund reality about Woolman's almost antiseptic views— a melancholia of sensitivity. Theodore Dreiser commented on Woolman's use of undyed clothing, "Nature uses all colors for beauty."[4] We agree with this comment and more, for we are ready to cry out with man stripped and exposed, with Shakespeare's poor, foolish, and finally tragic King: "O reason not the need! Our basest beggars/Are in the poorest thing superfluous" (*Lear*, II. iv.). Yet we must understand that Woolman saw clearly into the nature of man's self-will and the sources of his corruption. Instead of man waiting upon God, man waited upon Mammon. Woolman was faced with a problem in economics, therefore, as well as with one in morality.

Although not a sophisticated economic theorist, Woolman did attend to economic principles. Amelia Gummere, discussing Woolman's English journey, surmised that Woolman, pursuing "his way through the West Riding of Yorkshire," had made "a detour into Westmoreland with the evident desire to examine for himself conditions in the neighborhood of the great manufacturing centres."[5] Great changes in the economy of a people were taking place because of increased and more advanced methods of industrialization and because of the Enclosure Act which dispossessed so many small farmers from their land. Woolman had gone to England not only under the inspiration of traveling to the cradle of Quakerism, and to strengthen ties between English and American Quakers, but also to study the livelihood, the economics, of a people.

The details of his observations instruct us in the material from which he drew his theories. His shopkeeper's background was superb training for an economist: he records the exact price of rye, wheat, oatmeal, mutton, bacon, cheese, butter, firewood, rent, etc. Then he lists the wages of laborers, farmers, and industrial workers. And so he determines what the pay scale is in relation to the cost of the basic and minimum necessities of life. Woolman cannot forbear to write, "O, may the wealthy consider the poor!"

True economy for Woolman, as it was for Thoreau, was how much in human life something cost. Woolman viewed economy as a measurement of life, a spending of it. He observes in detail the hard, dangerous existence of the sailor, the seaman taking his four-hour watch in the "dark, rainey night," his return to the steerage "soaking wet," the unbearably crowded conditions, the foul air. And he speaks of the conversations among the sailors as they relate their voyages to Africa, how they brought the slaves out of Africa "in Chains and fetters . . . with hearts loaded with grief." For this commerce, "poor lads" were apprenticed to "learn the art of sailing." Thus Woolman writes, "In the Trade to Africa for slaves, and in the Management of Ships going on These voyages, many of our Lads and young Men have a considerable Part of their Education. Now what pious Father beholding his Son placed in one of these Ships to learn the Practice of a Mariner, could forbear mourning over him?" (505). The price paid in human life for excesses and luxuries filled Woolman with horror. The problems of "right livelihood"—the slaves or the Indians or the sailors or the postboys—was Woolman's chief and final concern during the last years of his life.

## II  *Ethical and Esthetic Considerations*

Having settled the question of "right livelihood" for himself in his personal life, Woolman now turned to develop the problem in his essays as one of how "labor answers life." We shall find in the essays that no matter what Woolman's subject, it is ultimately reducible to a problem of ethics. There is much truth to John E. Jacoby's statement, when he is discussing Woolman on labor, that "his method of treating the subject consists, as a consequence, above all, in exhortation. The underlying principles of it are, in fact, ethical principles, not economical."[6] To a hard-headed economist, this may be but another way of saying that Woolman is a naïf in economic thought. One nineteenth-century critic, David Duncan, said flatly that "he was not an economist; his views of life were determined by a narrow and restricted code. . . . He had confined notions of trade, and lived within a very confined circle of associations. . . ."[7]

Among Woolman's associates were the most brilliant and polished men of his time, and these included "captains" of industry and finance. As we know, Woolman himself had not given up without deep spiritual struggle the possibilities of acquiring

a fortune. Standing close to men of wealth, he measured carefully
the effects of riches. He himself was a landowner, a shopkeeper,
and a craftsman; he was well traveled, and he saw firsthand the
various ways in which people earn or fail at earning a livelihood.
Indeed, Woolman lived closer to the bone of life than most men;
and, given his high intelligence and wealth of pragmatic experience, it is difficult to understand why we should make a
provincial out of him—even if his theory of proprietorship would
not fare too well on the floor of the New York Stock Exchange.
I quote in full the following passage because in tone and subject
it provides us with the starting point from which we may proceed
to an understanding of the major ideas of his essays:

> The Creator of the earth is the owner of it. He gave us
> being thereon, and our nature requires nourishment, which is the
> produce of it. As he is kind and merciful we, as his creatures,
> while we live answerable to the design of our creation, are so
> far entitled to a convenient Subsistence, that no man may justly
> deprive us of it.
>
> By the agreements and Contracts of Our Fathers and prede-
> cessors, and by doing and proceedings of our own, some claim
> a much greater share of this world than others: and while those
> possessions are Faithfully Improved to the good of the whole, it
> consists with Equity. But he who with a view to self-exaltation,
> causeth some with their domestick animals to labour immoder-
> ately, and, with the moneys arising to him therefrom, employs
> others in the Luxuries of Life, Acts contrary to the Gracious
> designs of Him who is the true owner of the Earth, nor can any
> possessions, either acquired or derived from Ancestors, justify
> such conduct.
>
> Goodness Remains to be goodness, and the direction of pure
> wisdom is obligatory on all Reasonable Creatures: that Laws
> and Customs are no further a Standard for our proceedings than
> as their Foundation is on Universal Righteousness. (403-4)

God is the Landlord; man, the steward. When man acts the part
of the landlord, he becomes a mere usurper and causes misery.
Woolman thus strikes at the heart of laissez-faire capitalism, at
primogeniture, at the general inheritance of great wealth, at the
whole spirit of acquisitiveness; and he condemns an economic
system thriving on the foundations of luxury and superfluity.

In Woolman's day it was not uncommon—the Puritans shared

the Quaker view—to accept literally the belief that God is the owner of the earth. Today, more often than not, when we speak of God's earth, we do so metaphorically. Whether or not we derive fundamental economic principles from a belief in the proprietorship of God, the basic principle that "our nature requires nourishment from the produce" of the earth is the source of that immense complexity involving the production, distribution, and consumption of wealth—encompassing political, social, and geographical factors that we think of as an "economy."

It is a commonplace to speak of the "dignity of labor." Very naturally, we could not speak of it unless we voiced certain moral considerations that give meaning to the concept. By moral considerations, we mean something that goes back to the beginnings of time—to God's curse that man shall earn his bread by the sweat of his brow—and has to do with the "design of our creation." If we turn from the overwhelming complexities of our economic structure and its theological foundation that all productivity comes from man's labor in accord with God's injunction upon Adamic man, and study societies which are still in somewhat primitive conditions—for example the wandering tribes of African deserts—we would understand at once, I suppose, the meanings of how labor answers the "design of our creation." And it is in the rhythm of labor and creation that we may find the most illuminating considerations of man's moral estate, whether or not we see nature (and ourselves as part of nature) as having been created by God or as having been formed according to one of a number of scientific theories.

The question of how we live inexorably involves us in questions (perhaps unanswerable) as to the whole purpose of life. To say, as Professor Jacoby does, that the underlying principle of Woolman's "economics" is not really economics but ethics is, as I see it, not a harsh criticism. I take it to be a realization of the richness of Woolman's unsophisticated theorizing.

We may speak (not without humor) of esthetic as well as ethical and theological considerations. When Woolman's asceticism is formulated in terms of the "design of our creation," we are entering the province of the esthetic. Woolman, like Thoreau in his unwavering protest against superfluity, conveys a lovely sense of the cleanliness of natural, unencumbered forms; of the spartan lines of creation—an esthetic view. Woolman's feelings for the rhythm of labor and creation are artistic as well as ethical and, as incongruous as it may seem, "economic." The thought in the following lines makes us aware of an esthetic, as well as economic, view—"action," "exhausting frame," "fruit," "labour," "motion," "life" and "design": "Action is necessary for all Men, and our exhausting Frame requires a support, which is the Fruit of Action. The earth must be laboured to keep us alive. Labour is a proper Part of our Life; to make one the other in some useful Motion, looks agreeable to the Design of our creator. Motion, rightly managed, tends to our Satisfaction, Health and Support" (365).

If we remember that "action" coalesces into "motion"—that is, action directed by divinity becomes "motion,"—then we sense the harmony, the design of divinity, that Woolman seeks. If "harmony" and "design" may be explained as theological and ethical, it also may be explained as esthetic.

The problem with which we began—how labor answers life—may be talked about and is talked about in many voices. This is what we expect from Woolman. Although our emphasis is now on his "economic" views, we must not forget that those views are vitalized by belonging to a unity that includes God, modes of human behavior, and art.

## III  *"A Plea for the Poor"*

"A Plea for the Poor," once reprinted by the Fabian Society, is the most widely circulated and famous of Woolman's essays. The essay was printed in 1793, but it was probably written thirty years earlier. Woolman may have intended it as part of the *Journal;* it was inserted by him in the folio, MS.A, as Amelia Gummere informs us, "immediately following the incident with the Juggler at the Inn."[8] This episode, the stimulus for his essay, occurred when Woolman entered a public house to convince the people assembled for the performance of a juggler that it "was Contrary to the nature of the Christian religion" to spend money to support men in "vain occupations" (226). Woolman's attitude undoubtedly appeared as harsh to his audience as it appears to us. We may think, for example, of the medieval legend of the tumbler whose agility was all he had and whose feats before the Virgin were accepted by Her. In contrast to Woolman's rebuke, how much more humanizing and appealing is the legend. Naturally the somber qualities of the old Quakers (and the Puritans) disturb modern sensibilities; but, if we understand Woolman's attitude in terms of his theory of labor, we see how wholly human it is. After Woolman had spoken "in the fear of the Lord" to the crowd, a calm debate followed between Woolman and someone in the audience on the "reasonableness" of the view that the sleight-of-hand artist was, in his vocation, "of no use to the world."

The opening paragraph of the essay seems a continuation of the discussion, but the incident is not mentioned. We do not know what was said in the debate, but Woolman seemingly wanted to say that: "Wealth desired for its own sake Obstructs the increase of Virtue, and large possessions in the hands of selfish men have a bad tendency, for by their means too small a number of people are employed in things usefull, and therefore some of them are necessitated to labour too hard, while others would want business to earn their Bread, were not employments invented, which having no real use, serve only to please the vain mind" (402).

The opening paragraph is an overburdened sentence; it reads as if Woolman wished to say everything at once. Beginning with wealth and ending with vanity, the paragraph is concerned not with the poor juggler, but with "invented employments." The juggler in the public house at Mount Holly, as Woolman sees him, is a representative figure of wasteful economics. Although this rather narrow position of Woolman's tends to diminish our sympathy for his views, we are enlarged again by the rightness of what he seeks: the moral relation of labor to life. His point is that the vast inequalities in an economic system in which wealth becomes concentrated in the hands of a few fosters social conditions where the poor are exploited, by being forced either to work too hard or to labor in occupations which in themselves have no vitality or true purpose.

In either case, what is destroyed is virtue. A man cannot find "motion" in "action" if he is bowed by cruel labor or if he spends his life producing trifles for "the vain mind." Bruno Bettelheim's fine and often moving socio-psychological study, *The Informed Heart* (1960), deals with problems in our technological age which are closely related to Woolman's view of the cruelty inflicted upon men engaged in meaningless occupation. Bettelheim shows how men are often "seduced" by the triviality of contrivances—for example, the unthinking and persistent viewer conditioned day after day by the television screen—which destroys initiative and makes individuals passive; and men are also debased by work of no value, by "nonsensical tasks," which, in themselves being childish, reduce individuals "from self-respecting adults to obedient children."[9]

Thoreau, discussing economy, said: "A man is rich in proportion to the number of things which he can afford to let alone." This principle reflects the ascetic feelings that characterize Woolman as well as Thoreau, and I think both men applied it liberally to encompass the idea that a society is rich in proportion to the number of things it can afford not to produce. Thoreau also said, "Most of the luxuries, and many of the so-called comforts of life, are not only not indispensable, but positive hindrances to the elevation of mankind." In "A Plea for the Poor," Woolman talks often about "universal love" and "universal righteousness." "The elevation of mankind" has a pompous roll to it, and there are uncomfortable vagaries attendant upon phrases like "universal love" and "universal righteousness." Perhaps we react uncomfortably to these phrases because we are suspicious of admitting nobility into a corrupt world. The protest of Woolman and Thoreau against superfluities is one on behalf of "elevation," "love," "righteousness."[10] "The business of our lives," Woolman writes, is "to lessen the distresses of the Afflicted & increase the Happiness of the Creation" (405).

Woolman believed that the desire for wealth is the root of evil because in the begetting of wealth, luxury and vanity and power are born. The power that comes from wealth is always corrupt, for it is used in the defense of possessions. Possessions make the laws, hold sway, and govern. Exploitation, antagonism, strife, and war are inevitable outcomes of wealth as power collides with power in defense of possession. The inheritance of power and possession increases from generation to generation, and the end of life becomes the feeding of self-appetite. The gathering of riches formulates and dictates our customs, our opinions, our behavior.

Woolman examines a sacred concept in our society, "the rights of property," to see just what "right" means:

> The word *Right,* is commonly used relative to our possessions. We say, a *Right* of propriety to such a Dividend of a Province; or a clear indisputable *Right* to the Land within such certain Bounds. Thus this word is continued as a remembrancer of the Original intent of Dividing the Land by Boundaries, and implies, that it was designed to be Equitably or Rightly divided: to be divided according to Righteousness. In this, that is, in Equity and Righteousness, consists the Strength of our Claims. If we trace an Unrighteous claim, & find gifts or Grants to be proved by sufficient seals & Witnesses, this gives not the Claimant a *Right:* for that which is Oposite to Righteousness is wrong, and the nature of it must be changed before it can be *Right.* (425)

Woolman clarifies his position with an interesting example, an hypothesis really, in which he makes the supposition that twenty Christian men and their wives possess a discovered island. The land is divided equitably, it is improved, it is "multiplied." The pervasive spirit is love and harmony, and the government is a self-regulating body of men of good will.

If one of the original inhabitants wills the whole of his inheritance to a favorite son, one who is no more deserving than the rest of the "numerous sons," the favored son now has tenants—his "brethren and nephews." He has become a landlord. He insists that his tenants provide him with the necessities of life and even the adornments, the luxuries he feels he needs to support his "distinction"; and, "having the absolute disposal of these numerous Improvements, his power so increaseth, that in all conferences relative to the publick Affairs of the Island, these plain, Honest men who are Zealous for Equitable Establishments, find great difficulty in proceeding agreeably to their Righteous Inclinations, while he stands in Oposition to them" (426). There is now one landlord of increasing power living on the toil of his tenants.

In succeeding generations, by the time of the ninth or tenth generation of "landlordism," the heir is indeed supporting himself in "distinction." On the other parts of the island the inhabitants are living in peace and harmony. Woolman then says,

"If we trace the claim of the ninth or tenth of these great landlords down to the first possessor, & find the Claim supported throughout by Instruments strongly drawn and witnessed, after all we could not admit a belief into our Hearts that he had a Right to so great a portion of Land, after such a numerous increase of Inhabitants" (426-27). What constitutes the rights of property?

No man, despite the legality of his claim, has the *right* to more than an equitable portion. No man, despite the legality of his claim, has the *right* "to the whole, to dispose of it in gratifying his irregular desires." The oppressed held no "instruments" of legality; but "the Great Claimer"—Woolman's epithet for God is Whitmanesque—has given all men a right to sustenance without oppression or fear, and this is the higher right. "Thus," Woolman concludes, "oppression in the extreme appears terrible: but oppression in more refined appearances, remains to be Oppression; and where the smallest degree of it is cherished it grows stronger and more extensive: That to labour for a perfect redemption from this spirit of Oppression, is the Great Business of the whole family of Christ Jesus on this world" (427).

Moreover, the rich pass on to their children not only "outward substance" but molds of conformity which spoil succeeding generations. Thus the seeds of discord are sown. "A Plea for the Poor" is also compassionate in its feeling for the rich who have wasted their lives and the lives of their children on "outward substance."

Woolman's hatred of the effects of large accumulations of wealth and his belief that every man has the right to a fair livelihood have been misunderstood by the critics who would make of him a socialist. In *The Cambridge History* this statement appears: "Because of his candour and his fervour, Woolman might be called a socialist unconscious of his socialism, except for the fact that his efforts were exerted in a private capacity."[11] And in a widely circulated Fabian Tract, there is this piece of enthusiasm: "In his writings he [Woolman] enunciates, in simple religious phraseology, some of the truths which economists are only now beginning to understand: he is, as it were, the voice in the wilderness, the John the Baptist of the Gospel of Socialism."[12]

There is some but not enough basis for this view.[13] Nowhere does Woolman speak of the abolition of private property. His

objections are to "worldly pomp" and to an immoderate capitalism "where House is joined to House, and Field laid to Field,
till there is no place, and the poor are thereby straitened" (421).
There is no objection, for example, "for some to possess land, &
occupy much more than others" if they do not "on the Strength
of their possessions" oppress their tenants, their laborers, their
fellowman (424).

Nowhere does Woolman suggest governmental restrictions to
limit wealth. Rather, in his optimism, in his belief in human possibilities, he thought that if men opened their hearts to God they
would become men of good will. The economic practice Woolman favors seems to be a moderate, self-regulating, and benevo-
lent capitalism:

> Men who have large possessions, & live in the spirit of Charity,
> who carefully inspect the circumstances of those who occupy
> their Estates, and, regardless of the Customs of the times,
> regulate their demands agreeably to Universal Love: these by
> being Righteous on a principle, do good to the poor without
> placing it as an act of bounty. Their Example in avoiding
> superfluities tends to incite others to moderation; their goodness,
> in not exacting what the Laws or Customs would support them
> in, tends to open the Channel to moderate Labour in useful
> Affairs, and to discourage those branches of business which have
> not their foundation in true wisdom. (403)

"A Plea for the Poor" thus becomes an exhortation to the rich
to voluntarily exercise self-restraint for the good of all. It is
interesting for us to note the receptivity of the essay by its first
readers, the Quaker editorial committee, who changed the title
to the somewhat threatening "A Word of Remembrance and
Caution to the Rich."[14]

There is little in the essay that is threatening. The tone is calm
and reasonable. The essay is divided into twelve sections, and
each section is organized around a stated or implied homily.
Close to the heart of the essay, opening the theme of Chapter V
is a favorite homily of Woolman's, one that was used with great
effect in Part I of *Some Considerations on the Keeping of Negroes*:
"Ye know the heart of a Stranger, seeing ye were strangers in
the land of Egypt." Woolman describes the plight of the laborer
"who Toyls one year after another to furnish others with wealth

& Superfluities; who Labours and thinks, and thinks and Labours, until by overmuch Labour he is wearied & Oppressed." Such a laborer soon feels the burdens which are of "the heart of a stranger." Wherever the oppressed are, Woolman seems to say, there, too, is Egypt. If the rich "were to pass regularly through the means of knowing the heart of a Stranger" by changing "circumstances" with those who labor for them, "till seven times had passed over them . . . I believe many of them would embrace a way of life less Expensive, & lighten the heavy burthens of Some who now labour out of their Sight to Support them" (408). Woolman pleads for the awakening of "tenderness in the minds of all Reasonable people." He asks, and the question is rhetorical, "What heart will not relent, or what reasonable man can refrain from mitigating that grief which he himself is the cause of, when he may do it without inconvenience?" (408).

This view and the approach are antithetical to Benjamin Franklin's. Sometimes it seemed to Franklin that the poor must be reasonable and mitigate the grief they cause the rich. In 1768, in an article signed "Medius," Franklin attacked those essays which were sympathetic to the poor at the expense of the wealthy: "I have met with much invective in the papers, for these two years past, against the hard-heartedness of the rich, and much complaint of the great oppressions suffered in this country by the labouring poor."[15] The danger of "such writings" is they agitate the poor, and make them unhappy and rebellious. Moreover, such writings are unpatriotic because they give us a bad name abroad.

In defense of his position, Franklin states that the poor in the colonies are not so poor as the unfortunates in Europe. The rich are very kind, indeed, for legislating "a tax for the maintenance of the poor." Nor is Franklin convinced that the "poor laws" are a good thing. The rich, in voluntarily taxing their own estates, are encouraging the "natural indolence" of the poor. The rich have been most charitable—schools for the poor, hospitals for the "reception and cure of the sick, the lame, the wounded and the insane poor," and for those stricken by fire, storms, floods—and the poor should be grateful. Moreover, the rich lay heavy duties on foreign manufactures which oblige them "to pay much higher prices for what they wear and consume" in order to give support to the laboring poor. If the poor were not subject "to drink more and work less" every time their wages were increased, their situation would be much improved.

Although it has been argued by critics that the poor are starving, Franklin argues on behalf of the good accomplished by "luxury and expensive living." After all, Franklin says, "What the rich expend, the labouring poor receive in payment for their labour. It may seem a paradox if I should assert, that our labouring poor do in every year receive *the whole revenue of the nation;* I mean not only the public revenue, but also the revenue or clear income of all private estates, or a sum equivalent to the whole."[16] Franklin supports his position:

> The rich do not work for one another. Their habitations, furniture, cloathing, carriages, food, ornaments, and everything in short, is the work of produce of the labouring poor, who are, and must be continually, paid for their labour in producing the same. In these payments the revenue of private estates are expended, for most people live up to their incomes. In cloathing or provision for troops, in arms, ammunition, ships, tents, carriages, &c.&c., (every particular the produce of labour) much of the public revenue is expended. The pay of officers, civil and military, and of the private soldiers and sailors, requires the rest; and they spend that also in paying for what is produced by the labouring poor.[17]

True, Franklin admits, the rich may get richer by spending less than their incomes; on the other hand, some estates are diminished by the owners "spending more than their income, so that when the enriched want to buy more land, they easily find lands in the hands of the impoverished, whose necessities oblige them to sell."

As the argument continues, Franklin reiterates his basic point that the poor cannot ask for any more than they have since they already have *"the whole of the clear revenues of the nation."* His essay ends with the slightly humorous, famous, and nasty comment: *"Six days shalt thou labour.* This is as positive a part of the commandment, as that which says, *The Seventh day thou shalt rest.* But we remember well to observe the indulgent part, and never think of the other. *Saint Monday* is generally as duly kept as by our working people as Sunday; the only difference is, that, instead of employing their time cheaply at church, they are wasting it expensively at the alehouse."[18]

The difference between Woolman and Franklin cannot be characterized simply by saying that Woolman's theory of labor rests on a moral and Franklin's on a pecuniary basis. Franklin hated oppression in any form but often found himself speaking on behalf of oppressive authority. He believed in the goodness of worldly customs and opinions. He thought of wealth as a way to virtue. Crudely, virtue was something one could afford.

Surely Franklin would have agreed with some of Woolman's conclusions on the source of riches and the state of the wealthy. Franklin believed "the true source of riches is husbandry," and Woolman, too, was deeply committed to agrarianism. Nor would Franklin approbate those rich who lived a life of idleness, or those who maintained their positions by the labor of slaves. (Franklin thought slavery was unprofitable, but he also detested the whole idea of slavery on moral grounds.) And, although Franklin felt luxurious and expensive living to be beneficial to an economy, he believed more deeply in frugality. And, like Woolman, Franklin abhorred luxurious living that made for slothfulness of character. Woolman recognized that poverty could be a hindrance to virtue—as could wealth. A man must work and know what it is to harvest the grain for the bread he eats. Unless there be a "feeling knowledge" in a man as to what it is to labor, to answer, as it were, the "design of creation," the spirit of selfishness will possess him.

We find in Woolman an answer to Franklin's reasoning that the rich by living luxuriously support the poor: that is, they create new jobs. Woolman argues that, if we adhere to necessity, simplicity, and plainness in our lives, then we shall be able to establish a true "economy." We shall be able to shorten working hours by employing more men for the one job. Man would not be born to a life of drudgery, and workers employed in the production of trifles could find "virtuous" employment in the production of necessities:

Were there more men usefully employed, and fewer who eat Bread as a reward for Doing that which is not usefull, then food and raiment would, on a reasonable Estimate, be more in proportion to Labour than it is at present. For if four men working Eight Hours in a day, raise & clean three hundred Bushels of Grain, or twelve hundred pounds of flax, with Sixty Days Labour, then five men working Six hours and twenty four Minutes in a Day would at that rate do the same business in the same time.[19]

Woolman then turns his attention to the relation between wages and the cost of living. Prices being dear, wages are high. Because wages are high, "a large portion of Labour" is "expected" of the workingman. By employing more men in the production of necessities, the supply of necessaries increases, thereby lowering prices,

and labouring men having them at a low rate might ask less for a days Labour or a Certain piece of Work, & they working for low wages, their Employers might be satisfied with having less done in a day or a Week. In proceeding agreeably to Sound Wisdom, a small portion of daily labour might suffice to keep a proper Stream gently circulating through all the chanels of Society; & this portion of labour might be so divided, and taken in the advantageous parts of the day, that people would not have that plea for the use of Strong liquors, which they have at present. (409-10)

Woolman crusaded against spending time in the alehouse; but, while Franklin thought of drink as a cause of poverty, Woolman, as has already been noted, saw it as an effect of poverty. Man, as the steward of God (God's bounty was nowhere more manifest, Woolman believed, than on American soil), is to spend no more than "a right portion" of life in labor.

Woolman's discussion of poverty is not merely abstract or theoretical. In a dialogue between a "Rich Man" and a "Labourer," argument and theory seem altogether unimportant as the laborer describes how the poor "are often taught by moving instructions." The laborer's depiction of a family in poverty is piteously moving, and Woolman just avoids the sentimental. The family, faced with the problem of high interest rates (occasioned by the luxurious living of the rich) and of daily survival, has difficulty in providing for even their one poor cow: thus we get an extra dimension, as it were, as Woolman extends our sense of poverty into the hunger of all creation. The cow is so in need of grain and hay that "in her pineing condition, she hath called aloud. I knew her voice; and the sound thereof was the cry of hunger." Woolman, through the voice of the laborer, speaks of "small fires in long cold Storms," of "sufferings for want of fire-wood." What are arguments and theories? "In wasting away under want, nature hath a voice that is very piercing. To these things I have been a witness, and had a feeling sence of them; nor may I easily forget what I have thus learned" (462-63).

The poor have beheld "that fulness and delicacy" in which the wealthy live: "Those expensive articles, brought from beyond the Sea, which serve chiefly to please the desire of the eye, and to gratify the palate, which I often observe in thy family as in other rich families: these costly things are often revived in my remembrance when those piercing instructions arising from hunger and want, have been before me" (463). And these delicacies are paid for by exporting flour and grain; "Hence grain is more scarce and dear, which operates against poor labouring people." But Woolman usually finds the greatest economic evils wherever agrarianism gives way to trade. He had a deep and abiding antipathy toward commerce, as is seen in his "Serious Considerations on Trade."

## IV  *A Theory of Labor*

Benjamin Franklin, despite strong mercantilist tendencies, was, as we have said, fundamentally an agrarian. Of the "three ways for a nation to acquire wealth," Franklin listed war, commerce, and agriculture. War is robbery—the plunder of neighbors; and commerce usually involves cheating. The third way, agriculture, is "the only *honest way,* wherein man receives a real increase of the seed thrown into the ground, in a kind of continual miracle, wrought by the hand of God in his favour, as a reward for his innocent life and his virtuous industry."[20] Agriculture was, therefore, the way to a nation's productive and moral wealth. Franklin would have been in complete agreement with, even could have written, this line of Woolman's: "I know of no employ in life, more innocent in its nature, more healthy, and more acceptable in common to the minds of honest men, than husbandry . . ." (464).

Woolman's general point of view, as Joseph Dorfman discusses it in *The Economic Mind in American Civilization* (1946) "sprang from the complaint nowhere voiced more often than in New

Jersey—that the evils of the community flowed from the importation of luxuries." This complaint was used "even by conservative merchants to obtain the lifting of English restrictions on trade."[21] Franklin, of course, argued vehemently for free trade. He argued his principles on the grounds of prudence, but he also made it clear that he regarded trade restrictions as emanating from man's selfishness and as violating the natural (and providential) order. We do not know for sure Woolman's reaction to tariffs, but we know that he was for the imposition of one kind of heavy duty—an importation tax on slaves. The more severe the tax, the more it might serve to discourage the slave trade.

The success of trade in Philadelphia was all that a Franklin could hope for and a Woolman disparage. In the British Empire only London and Bristol surpassed Philadelphia in commercial supremacy, and the Quakers were amassing fortunes in overseas trade.[22] While Franklin was concerned with fair commerce and favorable balances of trade (a concern by its very nature that had to lead him away from an agrarian to a manufacturing emphasis), Woolman was worrying in "Conversations on The True Harmony of Mankind" about the debilitating effects commerce would have on his agrarian ideal:

> In rightly labouring for the true prosperity of a country, we do nothing at which any one of our inhabitants have just cause to Complain; but in putting forward trade beyond the right bounds, grain is made scarce and dear, even in a time of plenty; a poor labouring man must spend more of his strength to get a bushel of rie, than was required of him when less was sent abroad. Thus husbandry one of the most healthful, honest employments, so agreeable and inviting to us, is made a toyl, and becomes wearisome by reason that too few are employed in it, and too much labour assigned as the work of a day. (468)

Franklin, a complex figure with few easy consistencies, did understand and support the kind of position taken by Woolman even though he was an advocate of free trade. Recognizing the difficulty of obtaining a "fair commerce" where purchasers cannot know the fair price of goods, Franklin threw his support into the nonimportation movement and strongly urged that the colonists, through "industry and frugality," increase their "real wealth . . . even though no foreign trade should be allowed."[23] A healthy and vigorous trade, Franklin seemed to feel, could be maintained best where the state was strongly self-sufficient. He advised the citizens of Philadelphia to curb extravagances and superfluities. So it is that Woolman and Franklin became exponents of the same cause, agrarianism, although their emphasis, principles, and motives were far apart.

"Serious Considerations on Trade" was written in 1758 and published in 1922.[24] Woolman wrote this essay as a chapter for "Considerations on Pure Wisdom and Human Policy (1758)." The essay is divided into twelve sections or "paragraphs." Each paragraph—one sentence often forms a paragraph—conveys a simple and distinct idea and each paragraph builds on what has gone before. The Board of Overseers, as Woolman tells us, "did not reject this Chapter, yet [they] express't some desire that the publication of it might at least be defered" (397).

Woolman begins, as we might expect, with a divine injunction: "As it hath pleased the Divine Being to people the earth by inhabitants descended from one man; and as Christ commanded his disciples to preach the Gospel to distant Countries, the necessity of sometimes crossing the Seas is evident" (397). Trade, insofar as it is a bringing together of peoples into the family of Christ, is sanctioned by the spirit. Woolman also believes that new settlers, while clearing land in the wilderness, must depend upon trade for some of the necessities of life. But, once the land has been cultivated, it is important "that a Custom be not continued longer than the usefulness of it" and that there be a reduction in trade. For what began as a trade in the necessaries of life becomes, when this kind of trade is no longer needed, a trade in superfluities. It seemed quite logical to Woolman—and we must remember that in his day the crossing of the seas was a dangerous enterprise—that "where two branches of the same family" can supply their own produce and necessities, there is no purpose to be served in traveling "a large hazardous Ocean between them." It did not seem sensible to build ships and to risk the lives of men to satisfy desires for luxuries. We must be wary, therefore, of that trade for profit which takes men away from their true employ, the tilling of the earth. Trade carried on for wealth leads to "Sorrowful circumstances," and it "tends to increase the labour of such who fill the earth." Moreover, Woolman warns us, it increases the chances of war by creating mutual and competing interests among nations.

The luxuries of trade are the enticements of the rich. The laborer toils under the pressure of the tenant who, in turn, is forced to pay high interest to the landlord. The landlord needs high interest rates to maintain his life of luxury. By spending his money on superfluities, he creates a condition where the poor are forced into "vain employments." It would seem that the richer the landowner, the greater the increase in his demands as he tries to export more and more in exchange for "trifles."

Woolman observes that wages are lowered as the wealth and ownership of land become more and more concentrated. The profits from trade help the rich to get richer, but the poor have no "proportionable share in this prosperity." Woolman challenges the argument that trade "gets gold amongst us" and that all society therefore benefits. He challenges the value of gold and of currency as a true indication of and as a proper base for a nation's economy. Woolman's position has much in common with Franklin's, for Franklin believed the just measure or value of gold is labor. In other words, "a country's riches should be valued by the quantity of labor its inhabitants can purchase, not by the quantity of specie it possesses."[25] Trade is "the exchange of labor for labor."

In such statements of Woolman's as: "To make an axe or a hoe, iron and steel is worth more to the husbandman than gold of an equal weight," or the slightly caustic, "I believe the real use of gold amongst men, bears a small proportion to the labour in getting it out of the earth, and carrying it about from place to place" (469), we are dealing with an economic theory where value is measured by the purchase of labor.

Woolman believed that, if trade were carried on in a manner "consistent with pure wisdom," it would not be dependent upon the value of gold. "After all, if a man carried gold into those parts of the world where people are all strangers to that high value which is placed on it, and there endeavour to buy the conveniences of life therewith; to propose in exchange so small a piece of metal for so much of the necessaries of life, would doubtless to them be matter of admiration." Gold "appears to be attended with a certain degree of power, and where men get much of this power, their hearts are many times in danger of being lifted up above their brethren" (469).

The wealthy man is the honored man of the society. Money buys honor and creates the false goals, the illusions by which men live. A man, because of the honor accompanying wealth, feels the "inclination to rise up" and become as rich as his rich neighbor. To do so, he must resort to new "devices," even those which "may cause the bread of the needy to fail." Throughout the essays, the old and familiar text is preached in a variety of ways: "If Gold comes not rightly into our country, we had better be without it. The love of money is the root of evil, and while gold comes among us as an effect of the love of money in the hearts of the inhabitants of this land, branches rising up from this root like the degenrate plant of a Strange Vine, will remain to trouble us, & interrupt the true harmony of Society" (471). The greatest "interruption"— the one most emblematic of the disease of the whole economic system, of the discord sown in colonial society by the desire for wealth and luxury—is slavery.

It is altogether fitting that among the last things Woolman wrote was the essay "On the Slave Trade." There are no themes in the essay which we have not encountered before, for "On the Slave Trade" is a personal, deeply felt statement of a man at the end of his years who has devoted a lifetime to the abolition of slavery. "Under the Sense of a deep Revolt," Woolman writes, "and an overflowing stream of Unrighteousness, my Life has often been a Life of Mourning, and tender Desires are raised in me, that the Nature of this Practice may be laid to Heart" (497).

The worst forms of brutality have arisen from "ways of life attended with unnecessary expences." Woolman writes, "It hath been computed that near One Hundred Thousand Negroes have, of Late Years, been taken annually from that Coast Africa, by ships employed in the English trade" (496). Woolman speaks of "three or four hundred slaves" in a hot climate put into the hold of a ship, how they are frequently kept in "confinement" because of the fear of an uprising, how "distempers often break out amongst them, of which many die." And those who survive the voyage are abused by hard labor, poor diet, and physical punishment. They are grief-stricken for their homes and their old lives. It is no wonder that "some thousands are computed to die every year, in what is called the Seasoning" (497-98). Woolman listens to their groans, their cries. He writes with anguish of their cheeks "wet with Tears, and Faces sad with unutterable grief, which we see not" (502).

Woolman viewed commerce as an evil because ultimately one traded not in goods but in souls. He ends his essay with the words of Hosea, as if the grief-stricken Woolman can say no more: *"You have ploughed Wickedness, reaped Iniquity, eaten the Fruit of Lying, because thou didst trust in thy own Way, too the multitude of thy mighty Men."*

## CHAPTER 6

# The Journal, I

THE JOURNAL OF JOHN WOOLMAN is in large part the "witness" of John Woolman: "I have often felt a motion of Love to leave some hints of my experience of the Goodness of God. . . ." In Quaker theology there was no ritual or sacrament. For the Quaker, for Woolman most profoundly, life itself was sacramental. The taking up of "the burden of the Word," a phrase Woolman used, was in trust a sacramentalizing, a way of symbolizing the "signs" and "sayings" which bear witness to the Light. As the Johannine Prologue declares, "even the light which lighteth every man coming into the world."[1]

## I *The Esthetic*

When Woolman began writing, the Quaker journal was a convention, a tradition. Following definitive patterns, the journal had become institutionalized, a set way of recording Quaker history and of recording the spiritual life of the writer. Through history and spiritual autobiography, it became a record of the "experience of the goodness of God." From a literary point of view, perhaps we can understand best what Woolman was trying to do in taking up "the burden of the word" by a brief consideration of three texts: the Prologue to the Gospel of John, an introductory section to Robert Barclay's *An Apology for the True Christian Divinity*, and the closing paragraphs of Woolman's *Journal*.

We begin with the first proposition in John: "In the beginning was the Word/ And the Word was with God/ And the Word was God." This saying is then expanded: and the Word, existing before existence itself, as it were, is imaged in Light, the medium of spiritual life. Although I do not intend a theological exegesis of what might prove to be difficult and gnomic in the text, it is important to keep in mind, however, the suggestiveness of a relation between language and light. "'*Loquere ut te videam*': 'Speak that I may see you'," wrote Max Picard in his impressionistic study, *Man and Language* (1963). Picard has an artist's feel for this relation: "When a word is spoken, the air is filled with light. Language exists to bring light into the world." And Picard sees the light of language as not something to be "used." "It [light] raises words above the level of the purposeful to a place where language is undynamic, moving and shining in pure light."[2] As an example of this quality of light in its immortal and of course static form, Picard speaks of a Rembrandt painting:

> The light in Rembrandt's pictures does not come from the subject. On the contrary, it brings light into the subject. It is the light in which the subject has its origin. Rembrandt's light comes from the light; it is self-creating light. In Rembrandt's *Resurrection* the light that preceded language and the light of language itself are one. Language is absorbed by the light; the angel who stands within the light is merely a denser light. Light, angel, and language are all one. The inconceivable has here been made visible and expressible: everything is for ever but *one* light.[3]

For the Quaker, the "*one* light" is that of Revelation. "In the beginning was the Word." The light of Revelation, "the light in which God made the decision to redeem man," *is* the Word. The Word is more than conception. It is an embodiment, a symbol that participates in sensuous reality, as the second maxim tells us: "And the Word became flesh/ And dwelt among us/ Full of grace and truth." This leads us quite naturally to the supreme fusion of the third saying, a testimony and a witness and a declaration of divinity: "No man hath seen God at any time/ The only begotten Son which is in the bosom of the Father/ He hath declared him." The Gospel of John is an expansion of the thesis propounded in the Prologue, and it becomes so through the "signs and witness of Jesus."

The Word and the "sign" (often equated in the Bible with "miracle")—this is theology, of course, but also there are the implications of a high kind of literary theory and practice. The Johannine Prologue suggests a literal and holy relation between

divinity and language. The language of the Prologue is almost
magical in its repetitive effects, in its powerful incantation of
"Word" and "light" so that both are one, like the tonal absorption
and stasis in the Rembrandt painting. In the emotive mood where
language takes on a sacred destiny, where divinity and language
are made one, where divinity reveals itself *in the flesh,* in the
sensuous Word of life, then poetics and theology coalesce.

To read John Woolman is to go back in time when literature
took up "the burden of the Word." It has been said often and
truly that the colonial writer lived in a world of religious ideas.
A student of Puritan writings is well aware how consistently
these writings reflect the view that the visible world is part of
God's invisible workings, of God's vast ordination of the temporal.
That the visible world is but a fragment of the eternal world is,
as one philosopher observes, "a kind of naive platonism" that
"was the common possession of the colonial settlers."[4]

Woolman appeared at a time when the seventeenth-century
view was giving way to the rising empiricism promulgated by
political philosophers like the Englishmen Thomas Hobbes and
John Locke, the Frenchman Montesquieu, or Woolman's American contemporaries Paine and Franklin. God had become the
mechanic; the world, the machine. Our conventional image of
this deistic view of the world is that of the machine set in opera-
tion by the mechanic, the clock by the clockmaker, following
the perfect operating order of a mathematically ordained world.
At birth, the mind is a *tabula rasa* upon which experience writes.
In a world of scientific rationalism, we are no longer in a Providential world in any intimate or personal sense. In the diary of
Samuel Sewall (who died when Woolman was ten years of age),
we can follow the transitions taking place from a religious to a
more secularized society. But Woolman, aware of his empirical
times, reflected and vitalized the basic mysticism of the Quaker
testimony. There is a charm about Woolman's *Journal* in that
we watch the changes of the new age, the transitions, the natural
and reasonable secularizations, but something timeless remains—
Woolman's view—*sub species aeternitatis.*

The desideratum of Quaker purpose was set forth most com-
pletely by Robert Barclay in *An Apology for the True Christian
Divinity,* his classical, and somewhat Calvinistic, defense of
Quakerism: "What I have written, is written not to feed the

*wisdom* and *knowledge*, or rather *vain pride of this world*, but," Barclay says with a touch of defiance, "to starve and oppose it."[5] He admits at once that his style is quite different from that of common use, that is, "that which is commonly used by the men called *divines*." Barclay's feelings toward the "school-men" is not temperate. He confesses to being "an opposer and despiser of them as such, by whose labour I judge the *Christian religion* to be so far from being bettered, that it is rather destroyed."[6] Truth is of the soul, not of the intellect: "for what I have written comes more from my heart than from my head; what I have heard with the ears of my soul, and seen with my inward eyes, and my hands have handled of the *Word of Life*, and what hath been inwardly manifested to me of the things of God, that I do declare."[7]

The language of this statement, a conjunction of the spiritual and experiential, is in keeping with the suggestiveness of the Johannine Prologue. The "ears" of the soul, the "eyes" that are inward, and the "hands" that "handle" the Word of Life—no mere conceits but the Word made flesh, the words themselves being prompted, as Barclay tells us, by following "the certain rule of the Divine Light, and of the Holy Scriptures." And Barclay, too, declares himself a witness "of the things of God." Metaphor is no ornamentation; conceit, no brilliant polish. Writing must be true—it must be unadorned, as plain and free of ornamentation as the Quaker costume. All knowledge is derived from God— that is, we know by an inward seeing that conjoins the spirit and the flesh—and mysteries are made clear not by the power of the intellect but in the mystic brightness and rhythm of Word, Light, and Life.

This literary esthetic summons words to reveal to the heart the truths of experience; it is an evocation of words to reveal the never-ending, the perpetual rather than the historical, Revelation. Its inherent purpose was theological and its effect moral. The Quaker purpose was in some ways Wordsworthian—custom lying upon the soul with a weight, as Wordsworth writes in his great *Ode*, "Heavy as frost, and deep almost as life!"—in its search for light.

Like Barclay, John Woolman would not act "the Grammarian or the Orator," and if we were to look for a pervasive word that touches off his esthetic, it would be, again, "light." In the closing

paragraph of the *Journal,* where he is discussing the duties of
the ministry, Woolman writes:

> The natural man loveth eloquence, and many love to hear
> eloquent orations: and if there is not a careful attention to the
> gift men who have once laboured in the pure gospel ministry,
> growing weary of suffering, and ashamed of appearing weak,
> may kindle a fire, compass themselves about with sparks, and
> walk in the light,—not of Christ who is under suffering,—but of
> that fire which they, going from the gift, have kindled: And
> that in hearers, which is gone from the meek suffering state,
> into the worldly wisdom, may be warmed with this fire, and speak
> highly of these labours. (315)

The Quaker opposed mere rhetoric. Sincerity is among the
highest of literary values for the Quaker if we mean by it a
testing of the word and that which kindled it. Neither the word
nor its inspiration may be found wanting. At times this "plainness" militates against wit and joy and makes for a rather sallow
and somber style; but, with a good writer like Woolman, there
were occasions for wit, for bright clarity and bursts of splendor.
The Quaker style was necessarily plain: it was measured by the
rules of light rather than by the rules of rhetoric.

For Woolman, the use of words was no "adventure in dis-
covery," as R. P. Blackmur would have it, where "the imagination
is heuristic among the words it manipulates."[8] Art was not technique; it was primarily, essentially, vision. It is as if the words
were winged progenies of the archetypal *Word.* A Quaker sits
in silence in the meeting house until moved by the light that is
the Word, and then he has the voice. It is the Word that leads
him to meaning, not the arrangement of words that discovers
meaning. In Woolman's writings, no sparks warm us for very long
with the fire of rhetoric, nor is there the scientism of technique
that has so fascinated our age. There is, instead, a Christian vision
embodied in a well-developed and formularized Christian poetics:
Woolman, above all, attempts to liberate the ethos of love.

Woolman did not look upon himself as an artist; indeed, such
a designation would have been anathema to him! But he was an
artist; and he worked like one in his revisions of his manuscripts,
in his search for the right word, in his attention to technique.

He was an artist communicating successfully spiritual states of being, perceptions and attitudes toward the realities of experience.

The technique of Woolman, the mode of his saying, had been informed naturally by his tradition, but the power of his perceptions and attitudes was resident in the holy power of his soul. In Woolman was greatness, and it now seems inevitable that a great life, having felt the divine compulsion to write and having a literary convention in which to compose, would produce a work of high moral significance. *The Journal of John Woolman* is that work. It bears witness to the Incarnation of the Word as Woolman experienced the Word through the medium of light.

## II  *The Literary Tradition*

The Quaker journal, a distinct form of autobiography, shares with the Puritan journal the concern for a record of spiritual states of salvation, for a seeking of God's providence in worldly events and phenomena. It shares with the Puritan journal the desire to keep this record in prose that is simple and plain; but the career of the Puritan writer often seemed to be a preparation for death,[9] and at times his self-scrutinization—Am I saved?— bordered on the pathological. The Quaker writer, however, wrote for publication; his work was directed as much to the Quaker group as it was to an examination of his own experiences. Group awareness and the concern with successful living gave to the Quaker journal strong social emphasis. There was little regard for speculation about salvation, but this is not to say that the Quaker journal lacked introspection: "The seeking for divine guidance within one's being, in both major and minor decisions of life, naturally led to contemplative and introspective habits of mind. In endeavoring to follow the gleam, the Quaker became interested in understanding himself, and in turning his experiences of religious nature into a practical mysticism. This attaining of spiritual peace was not merely the result of a clear and satisfied conscience, but essentially of a complete submission of individual will to divine Will."[10] The Quaker journal, like the Puritan journal, was, therefore, introspective. The difference is in the nature of introspection—a question of what we find in self-examination—light or darkness.

Salvation for John Woolman lay in the annihilation of the "I," in a state of detachment in which the individual will merged into the divine. The way to salvation was love, love as we have distinguished it from natural affection. Love was made manifest in social action and divinity was bright in the moments of life. Jackson I. Cope, comparing seventeenth-century Calvinist and Quaker, writes: "And when the Light within gleamed unto salvation, it was not because man was crossing to join Christ in the Celestial City, but because Christ had risen again in man."[11] At the risk of over-simplification, I think it fair to say that the Puritan through this world sought the other world. But the Quaker sought the moments of immortality in this world. And literature reflects this immense difference for, "when the Quaker records his long travel from Babylon to Bethel, he exhibits none of the Calvinistic Puritan's minutely-detailed psychological percipience, none of his circumstantial narrative framework of names and dates and scenes, none of his careful recording of scripture, verse and chapter for each meditation."[12]

The form common to the Quaker journal has been studied and commented upon by many critics; but one of the best treatments is that of Howard Brinton who analyzed one hundred Quaker journals. He finds in them the following stages: "(1) Divine revelations in childhood; (2) Compunction over youthful frivolity; (3) Period of search and conflict; (4) Convincement; (5) Conversion; (6) Seasons of discouragement; (7) Entrance upon the ministry; (8) Adoption of plain dress, plain speech, and simple living; (9) Curtailment of business; (10) Advocacy of social reform."[13] Few journals contain all of these stages, and several may contain no more than three or four of them.

Woolman's autobiography is, however, a classic record of all stages. It would be a mistake to view these developments as steps of a ladder that are climbed one by one. The revelations of childhood haunt the mature Woolman, and the seeds of "convincement" are nurtured in childhood and in the period of his youthful frivolity. The quality of love, the great power in Woolman's *Journal*, coreces all incidents, all statements, all events and "stages" into a transcendent and wholly unifying pattern.

The "tradition" or convention which we are attempting to sketch grew naturally out of the common aims of the early Quakers and forcibly from the censorship committees which were soon established to insure proper promulgation of those common aims.

There is perhaps no quicker way of "creating" an artificial convention or tradition than by a tightly knit organization whose members submit freely to strict censorship. Louella Wright, in her excellent and detailed study of Quaker literature, sums up the work of the first censorship body of 1672: "In so far as the Morning Meeting checked fanatical tendencies, held the diction up to high standards, and helped authors to clarify the points at issue, it was beneficial; in so far, however, as this board stressed merely the interests of the group, it tended to hasten the day of eighteenth-century exclusiveness and of barrenness in literary activity."[14]

Woolman freely accepted the censorship of his work. Before sailing to England, he gave John Pemberton full power over his manuscript; and he knew that no line would be published that did not meet with the approval of Pemberton and the Publications Committee of the Philadelphia Yearly Meeting. Amelia Gummere's attitude toward the committee is temperate, for she reminds us that biography in Woolman's time portrayed the spiritual rather than the worldly life of the individual. Because of this, and because "history had not then become a science, and the historical sense was untrained, the eighteenth-century editor considered himself justified in omitting or revising at his pleasure."[15]

We know why Woolman wrote in the form that he did. Strictly speaking, it did not ultimately matter what was censored, for the full manuscript and its various versions are wholly recoverable. It is remarkable, however, that he was able to triumph over the strict limitations of form and content that made the Quaker journal uniform and even dull; indeed, it is remarkable that he could be inspired by uniformities and render to the form the vitality of life lived. True, it could be of value to have a tradition of form and subject matter as every reader of, say, Elizabethan sonnets knows. It forces the discipline and the joyous game of art.

The inner light, the medium of the Word, this, too, could permit a striking out, a way of transcendence. The great man could produce the great work in spite of the forms in which he composed. Also, there was one great advantage to traditional forms. Since the journal was a way of sacramentalizing a religion with no sacrament, the conventional mode and the peculiar language that had become cliché-ridden in Woolman's era takes on the poetry of sacrament: the present form and Quaker diction is always in essence a continuum and reminder, the sounding of the past. Indeed, in its attempt to utter the unutterable, to go beyond the rational, to transport us from the seen into the unseen, the visible into the invisible, in its incantatory rhythms and repetitive images, Woolman's *Journal* finally comes to share the qualities of poetry and sacrament.

## III  *The Plain Style*

A good deal of truth is in Dr. William Ellery Channing's statement, "The secret of Woolman's purity of style is that his eye was single, and that conscience dictated his words."[16] Perhaps it is because of this "indefinable purity," which Whittier also speaks of, "making one sensible as he reads, of a sweetness as of violets,"[17] that until recently an impression prevailed that Woolman was an untutored, a "natural," writer. Whittier himself says, "The style [of Woolman] is that of a man unlettered."[18] This kind of impression is a tribute to Woolman's achievement. That he was not tempted by the pen—that he was able to compose not for effect but for the lovely selflessness of conscience— accounts in some measure for his seemingly plain, effortless, unspoiled beauty of style. That Woolman was unlettered is, as we have seen, wide of the mark. His reading may not have been "broad," but he was a reader. We noted that Woolman, like most writers, did not simply write, but revised: there are three manuscript versions of the *Journal*.[19] And he was aware of himself as a part of the tradition which we have been discussing. Woolman read, wrote and rewrote, and followed tradition—he was not an unlettered and untutored writer.

We must, however, investigate the notion of the "plain" style. Fox, Barclay, and Penn were all advocates of the plain style, but this Quaker style was in many respects anything but plain. Quakerism had its own hard-fought-for vocabulary, and Quaker style was marked by a singularity of language. A host of peculiar associations came to surround certain words, and words seemingly naïve took on historical and moral contexts. It is correct to speak of Quaker plainness or simplicity of diction in contrast to the learned style of the schoolmen and divines, but we must not ignore the fact that Quaker diction has its own sophistication and learned qualities.

Thomas Clarkson, a non-Quaker and contemporary of Woolman, devotes several chapters in his pioneer history of the Quakers to what he designates as "Quaker language." A reading of Clarkson gives us a sense of contemporaneity reminding us that "as the Quakers are distinguishable from their fellow-citizens by their dress . . . so they are no less distinguishable from them by the peculiarities of their language."[20] If we take as an example the basic alteration made by George Fox of "thou" for "you," it becomes scarcely believable, as Clarkson says, "how much noise" this emendation made. Apologies were written citing its propriety —Erasmus and Luther were quoted in its defense. Objections were largely social. The rich and mighty were behind the objection regarding it as a degradation to be addressed in a way that reduced them "from a plural magnitude to a singular, or individual, or simple station in life."

Clarkson writes, "It was a common question put to a Quaker in those days, who addressed a great man in this new and simple manner, 'Why, you ill-bred clown, do you thou me?' "[21] For the words "Sir" and "Madam" were rejected. Master (mister) was also abolished. The letter of a Quaker would not end with "Your humble" or "Your Obedient Servant." All marks of honor and designation were abolished—"My lord," "His Excellency," "Your Grace," "Your Honour." The democratic ethical bent of the language, eliminating all class distinctions, is everywhere present.

So, of course, is the theological. The names of the days, heathen in origin, were called First Day, Second Day, and so on; for "Jehovah had forbidden the Israelites to make mention even of the names of other Gods."[22] So, too, the names of the months were changed; and, when Walt Whitman speaks of the Ninth-month in "Out of the Cradle Endlessly Rocking," he is not being "poetic" but a Quaker. And, because "Luck," "Chance," or "Fortune" had "no power in the settlement of human affairs," these words were not used in usual ways. Quakers did not use the expression "Christian name" because Quakers were not baptized and therefore not "christened."[23]

The point is there was an attempt from the beginnings of the Society to reform language, to bring it into accord with Quaker moral proprieties. Language was considered as "a criterion of religious purity."[24] Surely no movement in literature (except for the "New Criticism"!) ever held a more exalted view of the word than did the Quakers. The Quakers may say, Clarkson writes, "that the system of their language originated in the purest motives, and that it is founded on the sacred basis of truth."[25] Woolman writes, "If Christ is our Shepherd, and feedeth us, and we are faithful in following him, our lives will have an inviting Language" (510); and in the word *language* we now hear a special sound.

The plain style, then, is so by virtue of a somewhat sophisticated, if exalted, literary theory of simplicity which attempted to purify language, to get the right relationship between words and things, to establish a moral basis between language and being. In time, a host of associations have surrounded enough words and phrases that we may speak of a "Quaker language" and of a "Quaker style." To read John Woolman is not to read a simple, untutored writer; it is to read a man whose work represents the flowering of a noble, if at times tiring, literary tradition.

## IV  *A Gathering of Words*

Woolman's prose is often and most significantly a gathering of words and phrases of general scriptural usage and of more specialized locutions of Quakerism and mysticism. We have spoken of the Quaker journal as a spiritual autobiography and at the same time as a history of the aims of the Quakers. Woolman's language is admirably suited to express both the personal and the "group." The language of scripture, of the Quaker, and of the mystic was the natural language of his life. The triumphal fact is that his highly stylized vocabulary—which, we suppose, accounts for the epithets such as "quaint" and "archaic" that admirers like Lamb and Crabb Robinson have attached to Woolman's *Journal*—mixes freely with colloquialisms—a characteristic that seems to proceed directly from the heart of Woolman. The effect is unlettered simplicity and directness. Woolman selected, chose, and worried over words, but there is no affectation and no show: the language is genuine.

The recognition of an idiomatic and specialized vocabulary shaped by moral force is basic to a consideration of Woolman's style. Elbert Russell declared, "In reading some of their Quaker journals and epistles one almost needs a glossary."[26] Rufus Jones, for example, found that Woolman used the word "pure" forty-nine times in the specialized Quietist sense; for Quietism had its technical vocabulary. "Pure" is a case in point. Professor Jones defines the Quietist usage of this word:

> Nothing spiritual . . . can originate on the level of human reasoning. . . . Truth to be Truth, a message to be a spiritual message, must be given, must be communicated, and there must be nothing of the person himself supplied from his thinking process. It must come through "pure." The highest spiritual state for the Quietist is always "pure," that is, uncontaminated by any definite mental content. The word "pure" is, thus, a key word for the Quietist—"pure truth," "pure wisdom," "pure love," "pure life," "pure guidance," "the pure opening of truth," "the pure spirit of truth," "the pure gift of ministry, or of prayer."[27]

Altman finds that the word, like so many of Woolman's words and phrases, could have "ample scriptural warrant"; and he speaks of Woolman's use of "pure" as characterizing "the nature of God in His essence, the nature of everything which proceeds from God and the nature of man when he partakes of divinity."[28] Reginald Reynolds suggests the word comes from George Fox[29] but Altman thinks of it as a favorite word with the Platonists, particularly of John Everard, whose writings exposed Woolman, however indirectly, to Platonic thought. And Altman carries on the argument of usage to other possible sources.[30]

The same problems that arise in determining the meaning of "pure" arise in determining the meaning of many other words that are significant to a rich understanding of Woolman. The various ways the word "wisdom" is used, for example, or the phrase "motion and reality" suggest whole and singular concepts. Altman, who discusses the word "motion," says that it means "not an incursion of the Holy Spirit but a speaking within the person of the Divine element."[31] Altman sketches a history of the use of the word, and his observation that Woolman had changed the introductory phrase of the *Journal* "motion of Love" to "a desire of love" in one manuscript version warns us of the care we must take in the reading of a vocabulary that often tends to be specialized.

Another example is the word "harmony." Woolman writes early in the *Journal* that there is "harmony in the sound of that voice to which Divine Love gives utterance." In a later chapter, he describes his listening to the Indian chief Papunahung who speaks "with an harmonious voice." Of course Woolman could not understand what was being said, and by harmony he did not mean the mellifluence of the Indian tongue. What Woolman means is that love is present, that he has understood the source of sound; for harmony means the presence of divinity. It bespeaks a unity in which everything "fits." This gives to the word a vigorous reassertion of old meanings.

Even many of the standard or classical synonyms and epithets for Deity receive at times a special and most appropriate emphasis. We might expect the standard epithet, "Heavenly Father," when Woolman, "lying in the wilderness and looking up at the Stars," contemplates "the Condition of our first Parents when they were sent forth from the Garden . . . how the Almighty Being, though they had been disobedient, was a Father to them." Woolman next speaks of God as "the Father of Lights" (202). The epithet is natural, poetic, and summoned from nature. It is a less sophisticated and more literal expression of divinity than Heavenly Father, the kind of expression that has about it Indian lore. And of course there is an interesting and witty play in the contemplation of the garden, the Father of Lights, and the doctrine of the inner light which is always large on the page.

Woolman could be and was a fine phrase maker. Altman's favorite is "an affectionate regard for posterity," a phrase he finds as satisfying and as meaningful as Albert Schweitzer's "a reverence for life."[32] Generally, Woolman's phrasing and imagery are conventional, drawn from scripture or from his other readings. Pervading the book are such standard images as water for the spirit and for refreshment of the spirit, and fire for the might of God and for purification. He could and did use standard phrases in an interesting way. We might recall the dream images discussed in the second chapter, or we might take the standard phrase, "the well of living waters": "We took the meetings in our way thro' Virginia; were, in some degree, baptized into a feeling sense of the conditions of the people, & our Exercise in general was more painfull in these old Settlements than it had been amongst the back inhabitants. But through the Goodness of our Heavenly Father, the well of Living Waters was at times opened to Our Encouragement, and the refreshment of the sincere hearted" (166). The interest of "the well of Living Waters" is derived from the word "baptized," definition we must look for since the Quakers did not believe in baptism. Baptism and water are brought into conventional conjunction with ritualistic connotations while, at the same time, literally denying the conventional or ritualistic conjunction. I find the line essentially witty.

Woolman's style is also vitalized by his ability to sustain images, however conventional, in a series of passages and by the appropriateness of the image to the situation. The strength of his images is often derived from a strong sense of place. For example, upon his return from the back settlements of North Carolina, he writes of "the devoted" who find the "Divine blessing" that is "round them" to be "at times like dew on the plants." The images, although conventional, are fitting as men are made to "feel a concern over the flock." He writes of the "bloom of youth" and of being "seasoned" with truth. After a page or so, Woolman pleads, "And now Dear Friends and Brethren, as you are improving a wilderness, and may be numbered among the first planters in one part of a Province, I beseech you in the Love of Jesus Christ, to wisely consider the force of your Examples..." (198). Through the careful preparation of images derived from a sense of place (and of history), the literal and the metaphoric are conjoined—the backwoodsmen who are the first planters of a wilderness are at the same time the first planters of the seeds of light.

When Woolman is traveling to England and when he is in England, his imagery, again however conventional, reminds us continually of his isolation, of the three thousand miles of water between him and his homeland. A recurring phrase of which he makes prolonged metaphoric use is the biblical "the waters of separation." He becomes fond of expressions such as, "My heart was like a vessel that wanted vent" (314). His images, derived from a sense of place and arising from the mood of the situation in which he finds himself, have the power of transformation, the words moving us from place and situation into image, and image into the exaltation of spiritual fact. At a Friend's house, he refuses a drink from silver vessels: "Here I saw, that people geting

Silver Vessels to set of their Tables at entertainments was often stained with worldly Glory, and that in the present state of things, I should take heed how I fed myself from out of Silver Vessels." The literal becomes figurative; the figurative, a spiritual fact.

One of the striking things about the *Journal* is that, despite the generally quiet, spiritual temper of its lines, there is conveyed throughout the book a strong feeling of the physical. True, in large part, the *Journal* is the travels of Woolman; and his going from place to place provides, therefore, for the continual exertion of sheer physical movement. More than this, however, the imagery itself, through the sheer weight of accumulation, conveys a sense of the physical even in standard phrases. Woolman writes of men ministering "of that which they have tasted and handled spiritually." The spiritual is made immediate in physical sensation; the conceptualized is made visible. When the phrasing is not successful, the result might be an absurd simile, and we laugh.

For example, there is this passage written in England: "For several weeks at first, when my mouth was opened in meetings, it often felt like the raising of a gate in a water course, where a weight of water lay upon it" (314). The image is simply absurd. Fortunately, this kind of indulgence is rare. The usual physical interpolation takes the rather simple form of "tasting and handling" spiritually. Woolman, on the evil of too much rum, writes, " . . . it hinders the spreading of the Spirit of meekness, and Strengthens the hands of the more Excessive drinkers" (184). We know the "hand" is literally not strengthened but weakened— Woolman, we shall soon see, often summons the opposite of what he is saying. Not only is the hand of the drinker appropriate, but it provides the balance of weight to the invisible and ethereal "spirit of meekness."

Discussing whether or not he should venture forth into society when a smallpox epidemic is raging, he keeps before us the physical realities of infection. In his attempt to determine true motives for venturing forth, he asks, "whether aught of narrowness, party interest, respect to outward dignities, names, or Collours of men, do not stain the beauty of those Assemblies." The word "stain" awakens us to the reality of what he is talking about, particularly when he associates it with the word "body," which soon follows, and the word "blemish," which soon follows "body."

The words "beauty," "stain," "body," and "blemish" take on an associative reality and the disease, never described as such, is ever-present (228-29).

The sense of the physical is often associated with movement and particularly that of person. The following, seemingly artless development, is typical of the kind of word and line Woolman often uses. He is writing to a friend who has been under an "affliction," evidently an illness that appeared fatal; and Woolman says near the beginning of the letter: "We may see ourselves cripled and halting, & from a strong bias to things pleasant and easie, find an Impossibility to advance forward: but things Impossible with men are possible with God; and our wills being made Subject to his, all temptations are Surmountable" (185).

"Cripled and halting" and "pleasant and easie" make a nice antithesis—as do "impossible" and "possible," "Subject" and "Surmountable." Surely there is a neatness, a balance and antithesis, a rising rhythm, and even a perfect "physical" movement in sense and sound from the beginning of the sentence, "cripled and halting," to the rising, closing, and perfect word, "Surmountable." This paragraph is a summary of the message to his friend. He then elaborates and his method is the same: Woolman writes of the man in fear who is "unable to follow" the righteous as "deeply-rooted" and "unmoved" and "halting." And he progresses in this fashion to the final and well-wrought passage:

> There is a love Cloaths my mind while I write, which is superior to all Expressions, & I find my heart open to encourage to a holy Emulation to advance forward in Christian firmness. Deep Humility is a Strong Bulwark; & as we enter into it, we find safety and true Exaltation: The foolishness of God is wiser than man, and the weakness of God is stronger than man. Being uncloathed of our own wisdom, and knowing the Abasement of the creature, therein we find that power to arise, which gives health and Vigor to us. (186)

We are given a resolution, a final statement as to that which is truly unmoved—the "Bulwark" of deep humility. We enter the bulwark where we find the "power to arise." Our movement is characterized by "true Exaltation." The close connection between "Abasement" and "arise" gives us a feeling of rapid movement, and this is reinforced by the sense of exaltation, of freedom in our "stripping," as it were, as we arise. The relations between "uncloathed" and the abasement of the creature or the dissolution of the sensuous, worldly man and the love that "cloaths" is a fine play of thought and phrase. To the ailing man, Woolman is firm, optimistic, and comforting. To an ailing man, the phrase "health and vigor" may be oppressive. Woolman is inspiring and tactful as he renders into "physical" words a fresh, light spirit.

At times his word play is ineffectual and makes for the kind of bad humor that is one of the liabilities of the rhetoric of evangelism. Woolman, writing on one of his favorite subjects, the drinking of too much rum, plays on "spirits." In contrast to the "spirits" which man takes to revive him, there is the "Holy Spirit." And men take "spirits" because of the "selfish spirit" of those who oppress and drive them to drink (184).

We noted above that Woolman had a habit, at times quite effective, of calling forth the opposite of what he was saying. This is quite clear in the use of the word "outward." Writing of his brother's intent to travel with him to North Carolina, Woolman comments: "but as he had a view of outward affairs, to accept of him as a companion was of some difficulty." "Outward affairs" immediately calls our attention to Woolman's inward affairs. Altman suggests that, "In the minds of Woolman and his fellow mystics, there was undoubtedly a connection between the inward-outward dichotomy and the seen-temporal, unseen-eternal separation made by St. Paul."[33] It is interestingly, however, the temporal state—"outward wars," "outward habitations," "outward gains"—that evokes the spiritual and not the other way around. When Woolman writes of "a deep, inward stillness," there is no evocation of anything "outward." The spiritual state has the totality of exclusiveness.

And the image of the physical, in a special way, gives to the book a strange, pathetic quality. We can account for it stylistically by agreeing with Whittier when he speaks of the style as "making one sensible as he reads, of a sweetness as of violets,"; but there is, upon reflection, the abundance of that which Whittier does not note: the copious tears, the images of grief, of fatigue, of burdens, of weights, of bowedness, of stormy nights and dimness and darkness. There are the sheer physical discomforts: difficulty in breathing, failing appetite, nausea, illness, exhaustion; and there are trembling, physical revulsions such as the day in Newport where the slaves were put on sale.

The spirit of compassion that pervades the entire work in itself becomes an object of compassionate contemplation for the reader. Where the pervasive spirit is light but the sensibility is touched by worlds of darkness, the ensuing mood is pathos. If *The Journal of John Woolman* were all clarity and purity and light, it would be a book for angels but not for men. It is redeemed from conceptualism, from divinity, and from the "sweetness of violets," not by rank fumes, but by agonies of the loving heart and tears of humanizing concern.

## CHAPTER 7

# The Journal, II

EXCEPT for the first chapter of the *Journal*, the remaining eleven chapters deal at least in part with a journey or several journeys. The sense of journey and quest, the movement of a man under a burden, provides a general structure for the work, a broad thematic pattern, and at times the faintest touch of a large and grand, if not epical, quality. We are involved in continual movement from place to place. Sometimes we read a listing, a recitative of names, places, and distances. Sometimes we linger in a place. And if the events that happen are not subject to the whims of the gods, they are at least part of the plan of God. There are no celebrations of large heroic qualities, but there are the quiet ones that make for greatness, and there are dreams of prophecy and visitations of divinity. Pallas Athene does not appear before Woolman in the guise of a young shepherd, but a light of "easie brightness" shines in Woolman's dark chamber. And when Woolman writes of the voyage at sea, of the winds and the calms and the fogs, he speaks of God as "the Great Preserver of Men," and the epithet recalls for us other worlds.

## I *Structure and Voice*

In Woolman's world—one of movement and of stasis, of changing days and times and of divine moments, of high thoughts and of terrifying events, of the knowings of the mystic and the perceptions of the sociologist—the rhythms of style change at times radically and at others imperceptibly. Chiefly, Woolman has a fine way of working with the paragraph. Each paragraph has its own voice, its own syntactical construction because of its own impulse, its own thought. Sometimes we feel that we are at a Quaker meeting and that each paragraph is a speaker who arises and has his say and then sits down again. There is a pause, a silence, and another paragraph. What we have are rhythms of thought in paragraphs of thought. Quite often the rhythms are derived from scripture. There is an abundance of scriptural quotation and not infrequently a working in of scriptural language.

We can usually account for the variousness of mood, tone, and style. Sometimes a sharp change in pitch is necessary for our relief. For example, the most horror-filled narrative of the *Journal* is an account by one man of his captivity along with two of his fellows by the Indians. One of the men "being tied to a Tree had an abundance of pine Splinters run into his Body and then set on fire, and that this was Continued at times near two Days before he died. That they opened the Belly of the other & fastened a part of his Bowels to a Tree, and then Whip'd the poor Creature till by his runing round the tree his bowels were drawn out of his Body."

We are thankful for the somewhat calm and yet tender statement which follows: "This relation affected me with sadness, under which I went to bed; and the next morning, soon after I awoke, a fresh living sense of Divine love overspread my mind, in which I had a renewed prospect of the nature of that wisdom from above which leads to a right use of all gifts, both spiritual and temporal, and gives content therein" (269). Then the tone becomes more fervent, hortative, exclamatory until it does indeed hit a burst of holy passion. Then we may breathe easier again and go on with the account of Woolman's next journey; but what lingers with us as strongly as the evil of the captivity is the reaction of Woolman which overcomes that evil— he writes of love.

Occasionally Woolman's humor provides a change and a relief when the narrative has become somewhat labored. The following rather weighty and lengthy lines gather in strength only to collapse pleasantly in the final line:

Each of these Quarterly Meetings was large and sat near eight hours. I had occasion to consider that it is a weighty thing to speak much in large meetings for business, for except our minds are rightly prepared, and we clearly understand the case we speak to, instead of forwarding, we hinder business, and make more labor for those on whom the burden of the work is laid. If selfish views or a partial spirit have any room in our minds, we are unfit for the Lord's work; if we have a clear prospect of the business, and proper weight on our minds to speak, we should avoid useless apologies and repetitions. Where people are gathered from far, and adjourning a meeting of business is attended with great difficulty, it behoves all to be cautious how they detain a meeting, especially when they have sat six or seven hours, and have a great distance to ride home. After this meeting I rode home.[1]

His point is well made through the surprise of the final line, a poker-faced understatement after a windy line, a slight, wry note of grumpiness.

Then there is the voice which is divine. It is not only the voice which speaks the language of scripture, but it is also the voice of his dreams and visions. It is the voice that comes to him in great moments, of a "Sudden," as it happened when he was writing for his employer the bill conveying the title of a Negro. Woolman believed God "hath the power and command of all the operations in nature," and we are given on every page Woolman's sense of God's closeness to man, of God's immanence. All events are synchronized by God, and the appeal Woolman makes to the divine stirrings which he believed to be in all men and in the whole of the universe often renders what seems an indeterminate reality to the all too real events.

Grammatically, Woolman achieves the sense of divine immanence by an abundant use of the passive voice. Although at times the use of the passive slows and retards the sentences, it is usually most effective. Woolman views himself as an instrument; he is self-effacing; he is a man lead by the Holy Spirit. He waits in silence until he feels "that rise which prepares the creature to stand like a trumpet, through which the Lord speaks to his flock." And too, the passive often creates a quiet suspense; for we know that Woolman, once acted upon, soon will act. The use of the passive often "impersonalizes" the voice, and we listen to divinity as the voice sounds to us from a timeless distance. The paradox is that the self does not become incapacitated or dehumanized, but rather more discriminating, more imaginatively moral, more touching and humanizing.

*The Journal of John Woolman* is a devotional and religious work. Much of the freshness and delight, as well as the pathos of the *Journal,* is the play of opposites between the finite and the infinite, the natural self and the spiritual man, the worldly scene and the transcendent reality. The aim is the reduction of the personal, or perhaps more accurately, the expandibility of the personal until it achieves the annihilation of the impersonal. The self is expanded into the calm of absolute selflessness, of absolute principles. The transformed man is detached, liberated, unconcerned with theological haggling and doctrinal disputation. He lives according to the principles of love rather than of natural affection; thus, man is reborn to a new identity. That identity is to be found in obedience to the light and voice within him. The freeing of the slaves is the central activity of the book, and it becomes emblematic of the nature of freedom and of how all men must free themselves through love.

The motivation of the *Journal* being a motion of love, a divine "hint," the voice of divinity is ever-present, even though at times it may be, like Keats's melody, unheard. The voice of Woolman, human and compassionate, is also ever-present. The burden of the word is both human and divine.

## II  *A Myth of Harmony*

We have been saying that the religious mood is the dominant mood of *The Journal of John Woolman:* a mystic mode of cognition dependent upon passivity and Quietism. Yet there is probably no book in American literature that reflects a stronger democratic sensibility than this one. American writers and American politicians often compound (and confound!) the religious and democratic sensibilities. The contributions of the Puritans (despite a theology of the élite) to the shaping of American ideals has been well examined and acknowledged. The influence of the Quakers may have been equally as great. Their ideals were purer, perhaps because they were a more primitive people—that is, without dogma or doctrine—and the source of their imagination was direct and uncomplicated. We may think of writers like Whittier, or Whitman, or Melville who was part Quaker. They strike us in some ways as "primitives."

A world of Friends is theoretically a world of kinship, of total respect by each man for the mature and sensitized conscience of other men, of a simple and plain and basic equality. It is a world where there is no place for the willful and gross romanticism of the unbridled ego. It is a world of love, of selflessness, of tender concern for others, of "an affectionate regard for posterity." Woolman's religious faith is in this sense a democratic faith, one that gives expression to fundamental American ideals. The world he envisioned is a mythical world, as all political and social ideals combine elements of myth.

Woolman did not create mythologies or legends. He did not feel called upon to lend any myths to God. Yet, if we examine the repository of his ideals, we find in it the central "myth"—one that critics at least have made commonplace in American literature—of the American innocent and nature mystic, like Natty Bumppo (whom Henry Seidel Canby calls "the best Quaker in American literature")[2] or Huckleberry Finn. Man is free, sexless, and eligible for a particular kind of moral growth; and the tutor is the providential and sanctified natural order of unspoiled life in America. Woolman believed in agrarianism, worried about the evils of industrialism, and was suspicious of mere invention. If Woolman did not see man as a savage in nature or as a boy on a god-like river, he did envision man's noble estate as one outside of society in which man stood alone with God. Society was what one lived in; and one gave, as Woolman did, a life to the amelioration of some of the evils of society; but the great estate was one in which society itself became transfigured into some version of the "pastoral," where there would be no violence of heart, where wars are at an end, where justice and mercy reign. With Christ rising in the soul of every man, society becomes a self-regulating body composed of men of good will. Society is thus a religious state, but not a theocracy as we find it in the early Puritans.

The conjunction between man and nature that characterizes much of American literature becomes for Woolman the conjunction between man and God. The *Journal* is a book of social realities, and these realities, both good and evil, are transfixed by the eye of moral percipience, observations are meditated upon, hygienic exertion is ever-present, and the human is forever seen in the light of the divine, the divine in the light of the human. Just as the metaphoric and the literal slide into each other, so do the Utopian vision and the reality. Perhaps this gliding elusiveness contributes to our sense that reality, although fierce, is indeterminate; and, because of this, we get an almost ironic sense of the provisional nature of our world.

Perhaps nothing better illustrates the purity and mythic quality of Woolman's society than his attitude toward the brute creation. There was the famous incident of his boyhood—the stoning of the robin and the killing of her young. We remember Woolman's reaction to this incident and how it made him aware of his kinship with all creation. And in the last few months of his life, when he was enroute to England, he observed the condition of the fowl which had been taken by some of the passengers for their "Sea-store." He observed the fowls' "dull appearance" and their "pineing sickness." As the small always suggests to Woolman the great, he thinks of God "who gave being to all creatures, and whose love extends to caring for the sparrows." This concept leads him to contemplate upon "the true Spirit of government" where "a tenderness toward all creatures made Subject to us will be experienced & a care felt in us that we do not lessen that Sweetness of life in the animal Creation which the great Creator intends for them under our government" (302). The tone of the statement does not suggest conservationism or humane shelters, but something grander—the image of Adamic man (in undyed clothing) frolicking with the animals. The concept is a throwback to the primitive imagination, the Edenic dream of a government not of man alone, but a government of man and animal, a myth of Oriental harmony, of "Sweetness of life" in all creation.

### III  *A Language Not of Words*

The temporal and yet the emergent timelessness of Woolman's world, the sensation of place and yet the ultimately imaginative and meditative nature of place, is analogous to the same kind of seeming paradox of the Word in John: the Word of creation and the Word that existed before creation. We are dealing finally, of course, in symbolic realities. Woolman, we said, viewed life as sacrament. Life itself is "language"; life as sacrament is living the language of the unutterable. Another way of explaining it, perhaps, is to say that "reality" is linguistic and that ultimate reality is eternal silence bringing us back to the Word itself which existed before all creation. As Paul Tillich suggests, without the

Word, there are no possibilities for life and history; life and history are, therefore, "linguistic orders."[3] It is in this sense, I think, that the saying, "And the Word became flesh," may be understood as a symbolic mode of shattering the silence that we cannot know linguistically. God does not speak "words."

When Woolman is "visited" with Certain Evidence of Divine Truth, and it is significant enough to quote in part again, he writes of seeing the light in his chamber: "As I lay still without any surprise looking upon it, words were spoken to my inward ear which filled my whole inward man: They were not the effect of thought, nor any conclusion in relation to the appearance, But as the language of the Holy One Spoken in my mind: the words were *Certain Evidence of Divine Truth,* and were again repeated exactly in the same maner, whereupon the light disappeared" (187). I think it clear that the language was not a language of words but of unfathomable silence. There is no logical context to which words can be referred—"they were not the effect of thought, nor any conclusion in relation to the appearance." Words speak through light just as God spoke to Moses through a burning bush, or, just as God, through an angel, touched the lips of Isaiah with a live coal.

As light urges us into language, so language urges us back into the silence from which it came. We come back to the "inner light," the "inner voice," or the "logos"—another way of saying that we come back to a "deep inward stillness." The *Journal,* finally, is a symbolic mode of shattering the silence, an utterance of the unutterable, like all sacrament. Its attempt is to liberate us by making visible the forms of stillness or by rendering flesh to spirit—the great attempt, it seems to me, of all serious art. In the issuing forth and the coming back to silence, we may think of the Quaker in the quiet of the meeting house who feels a "motion" or "concern." He rises, he feels voices speaking through him, he gives utterance to these voices, and then he sits and returns again to a deep inward stillness. Or we might think of that fine passage in *The Confessions of St. Augustine:*

To Thee therefore, O Lord, am I open, whatever I am; and with what fruit I confess unto Thee, I have said. Nor do I confess it with words and sounds of the flesh, but with the words of my soul, and the cry of the thought which Thy ear knoweth. For when I am evil, then to confess to Thee is nothing else than to be displeased with myself; but when holy, nothing else than not to ascribe it to myself: because Thou, O Lord, blessest the godly, but first Thou justifieth him when ungodly. My confession then, O my God, in Thy sight is made silently, and not silently. For in sound, it is silent; in affection, it cries aloud. For neither do I utter anything right unto men, which Thou hast not before heard from me; nor dost Thou hear any such thing from me, which Thou hast not first said unto me.[4]

Men must use words among men; but, in communion with God, the voice is within, filling the whole inward man, as Woolman says; and there is silence. For God has placed the Word within the soul, and only in silence is our full realization of it possible.

The qualities of which we are speaking give a depth to *The Journal of John Woolman;* beside it, *The Autobiography of Benjamin Franklin,* the other and more popular autobiographical classic of prerevolutionary America, seems shallow. The reason is that in Franklin the "logos" or "voice" has become thoroughly secularized, has been made reason or common sense. In Franklin's *Autobiography,* there are no manifestations, divine or otherwise, beyond the rationality of its clearly ordered and simple prose. This is probably what D. H. Lawrence had in mind when he spoke of Franklin as taking away his "wholeness," his "dark forest," "his freedom," that is, his "illimitable background." The Gods, Lawrence said in his *Studies in Classic American Literature,* must "come forth from the forest into the clearing of my known self and then go back. That I must have the courage to let them come and go." For Woolman, it was voices from the light or the stillness; but man's freedom did come from an "illimitable background."

Franklin leaves us with no sense of the mystery of life as does Woolman, but he gives us a method to bring some order out of the muddle of life. In Franklin's *Autobiography* we have words without silence, and little more than the story of an enlightened, self-made, admirable man. The eternal silence of infinite space which struck terror into Pascal does not exist for the Franklin of the *Autobiography.* Franklin experimented in space with kites and lightning rods, but never, except pragmatically, did the void touch his genial heart.

Jonathan Edwards, like Woolman, was a mystic. Henry Canby

suggests, however, that a comparison of Woolman's writings with Edwards' *Freedom of the Will* would reveal fascinating temperamental divergencies not unlike those we find between Shakespeare and Racine.[5] I suppose Canby means that the emphasis in Woolman is on the potentialities of man in this world; in Edwards, on the limitations of man in this world. (Racine was a Jansenist, and there was a good deal of Calvinism in Jansenism). Perhaps, too, Canby has in mind Edwards' logic and high formalism that seem belated and divorced from the realities of his time. It might be more to the point to compare Edwards' brief spiritual autobiography, *A Personal Narrative* with Woolman's *Journal*, for it is more nearly mystical and more openly psychological than the somewhat dry rationalism of *Freedom of the Will*. In *A Personal Narrative* there is a turbulence sharply contrasting to the general calm of the *Journal*. There is in Edwards a loving and ravishing of God that at times recalls to us the ecstatic in Richard Crashaw or even George Herbert. Woolman recalls to us the sane humanism and poise of Jeremy Taylor.[6]

Often we find in Edwards the signs of a great and tragic lover —moods of inexpressible beauty in which we taste the honey of paradise and those of torment that seem to heat the very fires of hell. Like Woolman, Edwards struggled for acquiescence, for that kind of abasement of the creature which we call "humility." Edwards thus tries to take us into silence, but he cannot rest; his passion, his stillness, and his humility finally become orders of logic. In Edwards rationalism triumphs over intuition. There is nothing logical to which we can refer either intuition or silence. There comes to mind a poem of Emily Dickinson's that reads, "By Intuition Mightiest Things/ Assert themselves—and not by terms." And in another poem, she writes:

> Great Streets of Silence led away
> To Neighborhoods of Pause
> Here was no Notice—No Dissent
> No Universe—no Laws—

The unutterable has no context; silence, no face. "When Bells stop ringing"—again Emily Dickinson—"Church begins." And so it does for the Quaker Woolman, but not for his Calvinist contemporary. When the bells stop ringing for him, the day of doom has arrived.

## IV *Woolman and Dreiser*

It is almost a commonplace to suppose that at the outbreak of the American Revolution, the two men most representative of our apparently irreconcilable "cultural identities"—our divided sects and opinions—were Jonathan Edwards and Benjamin Franklin. In the Puritanism of Edwards is embodied the moral idealism pervasive in much of American thought, certainly Emersonian thought. In the secularized Puritanism of Franklin is embodied the sagacity of that idealism when it is reasonably applied to utilitarian or social concerns. Edwards in the eighteenth century invigorated and gave a momentary, life-like splendor to the apostolic trance of his seventeenth-century forefathers; Franklin, depuritanized into Deism, suggests the mechanical power and prosperous being of America in the second half of the twentieth century. Both men of the Enlightenment, they have become—for better or for worse, erroneously judged or not—symbolic of the fundamental antagonisms of their time.

In Woolman, there is left a heritage that is conjunctive with the passionate spiritual idealism of Edwards and with the deeply social and humanitarian concerns of Franklin. It is of more than casual interest that Woolman records his first appearance in the vocal ministry in the year 1740-41, the year of that colossal religious revival, the Great Awakening, when, for several months, Jonathan Edwards "was the most powerful man on the continent."[7] It is interesting, too, as we have noted, that the publisher of Woolman's anti-slavery tract, *Essay on Considerations on Keeping Negroes* (1762), was Benjamin Franklin. Associations of this kind suggest more than they support, but they do have a teasing interest for ingenuous criticism.

Indeed, it might take much ingenuity to discuss Woolman as a major influence in literature. In Woolman's impact upon men like Samuel Taylor Coleridge, Charles Lamb, Crabb Robinson, Channing, and Emerson—to name a few—we have a touchstone for the quality of his achievement. It seems, however, that not until the twentieth century was Woolman's influence directly felt by a major writer—Theodore Dreiser.

Without Dreiser's emerging consent to Quaker ideals, if not religion, *The Bulwark* (1946), his final novel, could not have been written. In a letter to Rufus Jones, December 1, 1938, Dreiser wrote, "As you know I am very much interested in the Quaker ideal. Like yourself I rather feel that it is the direct road to—not so much a world religion as a world appreciation of the force that provides us all with this amazing experience called life."[8] Woolman's *Journal* provided much of the inspiration for the book, perhaps its very conception. Reading the following passage in Rufus Jones's *The Trail of Life in the Middle Years* (1934), Dreiser wrote in the margin of the page the name of the hero of *The Bulwark*, "Solon": "Woolman expresses, both in spirit and in deed, better than any other single individual does, the ideal of Quaker mysticism. He carried farther than most have done the refining process which consumes the dross in cleansing fire, and leaves the spirit pure and unalloyed, utterly humble, and utterly freed from selfishness."[9]

And, in his introduction to his edition of Thoreau, Dreiser wrote,

He [Thoreau] reminds me of some of the most arresting characters in history whether it be Diogenes with his lantern, Christ with his dismissal of all thought for tomorrow—what ye shall eat or what ye shall wear—Buddha, walking from his palace to a bo tree, St. Francis with his imitation of Christ, Thomas à Kempis likewise, or, to come nearer our own time, John Huss, John Fox, John Bunyan, John Woolman. All these men were arrested by the beauty and mystery of life, the joy and the pain, the ignorance and the wisdom, the good and the evil, the birth and the death.[10]

In the following passage, Dreiser attempts, in writing about Thoreau, to define a little more closely the specific relation between Thoreau and Woolman: "In common especially with the Transcendentalists as well as with many other moral and romantic philosophers, he can be said to share these two beliefs, (1) that solitary contemplation of nature brought a harmony with the spiritual force which created the world, and (2) that what is right is so by reference to intuition. Of course, John Fox has that thought and after him the Friends or Quakers. Also John Woolman, whom, in many of his solitary communion deductions, Thoreau resembles. Also Buddha, Jesus, Lao-Tze."[11]

Finally, Dreiser recommended to the Dean of Whittier College that Woolman's *Journal* be required reading, for it would offer "the greatest service and encouragement for all seeking an intelligible faith."[12] (Amelia Gummere writes, "The *Journal* was at one time in use as a text book at Princeton University, for the purity of its English, and in 1920 the State of Pennsylvania required it of its candidates in the public school examinations").[13] There was much about Woolman that Dreiser would naturally admire: Woolman was always on the side of the poor and the oppressed. He combined social conscience and action with a strong philosophical idealism. The philosophical idealism that had always been inherent in Dreiser's thought, however vaguely and sentimentally it had been expressed, could be related to political, social, and economic thought and action. Woolman provided the example.

Dreiser borrowed freely from the *Journal*. The stoning of the robin, which we discussed earlier, constitutes the whole of Chapter Four in *The Bulwark*. Dreiser added the Naturalistic touch of a Darwinian world, the law of nature feeding on nature, to his retelling of the incident: Solon Barnes kills a bird with a slingshot; and Tommy Briggam, Solon's companion, takes the dead bird and the nest of her young home to the cat. Woolman's work is mentioned several times, and young Solon Barnes finds the *Journal* "interesting to read, since it contained the story of an extraordinary man's life, and, as a connected narrative, was easier to follow than the Bible or the Book of Discipline." There are numerous other incidents where Dreiser's debt is evident. One is the characterization of Solon's father as a man who, in conducting business, "was frequently moved, particularly in the instance of customers whom he knew to be at best eking out a meager existence, to inquire; 'What is it thee intends to do with it, John?'" And Rufus Barnes would save the buyer money, just as Woolman did. And practically the whole of Chapter Sixty-six is based on and contains a lengthy text from the *Journal*. And certain techniques, like "frameworks" of illness and recovery are found in the *Journal*.[14] Dreiser even quotes from Whittier's introduction to the *Journal*.

Woolman's influence may be felt also in what is for Dreiser a rather lean style of his last novel. As F. O. Matthiessen observed, "It [*The Bulwark*] does not have his usual documentation, his thorough, heavy immersion in details." In defense of the charge that Dreiser's style in *The Bulwark* "has appeared plain to the point of thinness," Matthiessen answers that "We can judge the effect of the whole only if we realize that it is far more a symbolical than a naturalistic novel, basically as bare as a parable."[15] Sidney Richman, in his study, says that "Dreiser was simply illustrating in his new style and conception of the novel the major distinction between the naturalist and the literary mystic."[16] I think Woolman's *Journal*, simple and plain, sparing of details, and highly symbolic (spiritualized), had a strong influence on Dresier's style.

*The Bulwark* is not a great success, and the chief cause was Dreiser's inability to convey in the novel the quality of love. The love Woolman writes about becomes in Dreiser literary, intellectual, and often sentimental; moreover, Dreiser also confused Thoreau's views of nature with Woolman's. Nor is it enough to capture a mystique of nature by mere poetics. What must be grasped and felt ultimately is the paradox and the glory expressed in Eliot's "Ash Wednesday":

> Against the Word the unstilled world still whirled
> About the centre of the Silent Word.

Dreiser intellectualized, listened to and was deeply influenced by Woolman's voice; but he had no true understanding of the silence from which it came.

## CHAPTER 8

# The Journal, III

A T THE CONCLUSION of the *Journal*, Woolman describes himself as a man who has "gone forward, not as one travelling in a road cast up, and well prepared, but as a man walking through a miry place in which are stones here and there safe to step on; but so situated that, one step being taken, time is necessary to see where to stop next." We may detect a perspective and something of a humorous conjuration in the relation of this line to the one that follows: "Now I find that in pure obedience the mind learns contentment in appearing weak and foolish to the wisdom which is of the world" (315). If we literalize the image of a man fixed for a time on a stone in the midst of mire, wondering where to stop next, we find in the picture a foolishness of sorts, particularly if we see the man on the stone reasoning, gesticulating, evangelizing, crying forth, and quietly listening. The image becomes all the more incongruous when we describe the *Journal*, as we have described it, as a journey, a quest. There is a hint of romance in the movement of a man under a burden, but romance is transformed to the comic if we think of the movement as being as deliberate as stone-stepping through mire.

## I *The Law of Omission*

This final image of himself is one of unfeigned humility and unwitting humor. Woolman's unposed presence is an interesting commentary on his regard for the self, and it forms a significant contrast to the image posed by Thoreau in *Walden*. The image of Thoreau's struggle is a "slight and graceful hawk," alone but not lonely, "sporting" in the sky, and making "all the earth lonely beneath it." Originally, Thoreau thought of the butterfly emerging from the larvae state to symbolize the nature of his struggle and victory, but at the end he identified with the "proud reliance" of the hawk.[1] And Walt Whitman also expresses a marvelous confidence in the self. In the closing lines of *Song of Myself*, he portrays the self as spontaneous and joyful, infinitely expansible and contractible, stopping somewhere to wait for us. "You will hardly know who I am or what I mean," Whitman writes in his closing lines, "But I shall be good health to you nevertheless."

Thoreau lived through more than one winter of discontent, and Whitman knew what it was to "look out upon all the sorrows of the world" and to sit in agony and be silent. However, like Emerson, they both believed man was of the buoyant earth and that man stood in the center of the universe. They believed the possibilities of man were infinite; and, in this respect, the American renaissance was the heir of the Renaissance. The streams of creation converged to meet in the breast of every man to form a soul. The self could not escape the drama of its own importance. It became a *poseur*, an actor who could play brilliantly, if it so willed, a bewildering variety of roles. In Whitman the self could become even a most hardy and robust Christ touched with human bravado. We may think of Emerson's beautiful and forever haunting description of man as a god in ruins. And then there is Thoreau's ideal, somewhat detached and effete in the final analysis, of the artist of Kouroo carving his perfect stick while about him the eras pass and dynasties fall. In Woolman we find no bravado, no lament, no intellectual pale—and certainly no multiplicity of roles or changing identities.

F. O. Matthiessen, speaking of Bronson Alcott's failure "to convey the impression of a thing clearly seen or wholly experienced," accounts for it and the general failure of Transcendentalists (Thoreau excepted) to emerge from their Transcendental "vapor": "In mystical literature, no less than in other types, the manner of writing is organically dependent upon the strength and lucidity of the vision. The concrete firmness of an Edwards or a Woolman even in communicating what lies beyond the senses is one indication of what the transcendentalist lost by giving up the modes of traditional piety in order to assert the divineness of himself."[2] For Woolman, the trusteeship of the self, as we have observed, is the Word within, the Divine light, "even the light which lighteth every man." The self in passive obedience to the Word thus becomes instrumentalized. Its beauty and drama is in its sound and finally in the reflective note of sound that turns us inward and induces silence, and, if we will, devotion.

But Woolman's is not the self as doer, the self which we find epitomized in Emerson's "Self-Reliance" as "A sturdy lad from New Hampshire or Vermont, who in turn tries all the professions, who *teams it, farms it, peddles,* keeps a school, preaches, edits a newspaper, goes to Congress, buys a township, and so forth, in successive years, and always like a cat falls on his feet," that carries the burden of the word. It is true a man may do all of these things—Woolman did a few of them—but we are talking about differences in the sources of action which make the man and which naturally determine the principles and temper of action.

In Emerson, Thoreau, and Whitman, the safeguards for the self remain nebulous or perhaps so diffuse as to be finally nebulous. Matthiessen believed that Thoreau was "saved" from the Transcendental fate of "looseness and abstractness" by "his awareness of the shift in the object of his worship." That shift was to the constancy of "Pan."[3] Yet, I find that Thoreau's democratic, self-reliant man crowing lustily like Chanticleer under the trusteeship of Pan has a comic element about it. In general, the Romantic tendency to make gods of men is one of the amusing paradoxes and frightening dangers of Romanticism and is a challenge in obvious ways to the egalitarian impulse of the great Romantic movements.

Woolman was too much of the Enlightenment and too much the Quaker to think of man as a god, although divinity was in man. Yet, he was a progenitor of social revolution. Neither Emerson, Thoreau, nor Whitman were as practically and directly influential in any great historical cause of their time as was Woolman in his struggle for the abolition of slavery. Indeed, former Senator Paul Douglas of Illinois thinks of Woolman as the co-founder, along with Pastorius, of the Abolition Movement in America.[4] Woolman was Emerson's self-reliant man, but the difference—and it made for radical differences—was that the "I" could not burst forth unbridled and undisciplined because there was nothing nebulous about the trusteeship of the self: the trustee is the Christ within. Woolman's bulwark was a humility that derived from total belief in the unorthodox theology of a radical faith.

Thoreau called Quakerism "a mild form of transcendentalism." Transcendentalism, in part an attempt to reconstruct a faith out of a shattered Unitarianism, had no "testimony," no Book of Discipline, no meeting house. Despite the perjorative intent of Thoreau's description of Quakerism, the kinship between the Quakers and the Transcendentalists is marked and close. Discussing Emerson's thought that "perception is not whimsical, but fatal," Matthiessen writes: "The doctrine hinted there is what Thoreau and Whitman also relied on. It involves a mystical acceptance of intuition as final, and demands an unswerving loyalty to its dictates. It discloses what Emerson meant by his frequent remarks that he felt more kinship with the inner light of the Quakers than with any formal creed."[5] And of Whitman, Matthiessen says: "The sympathetic kinship that Emerson felt with Quakerism in his liberated maturity had belonged to Whitman as his birthright."[6] Matthiessen cites the influence of Elias Hicks on Whitman, the qualities of Whitman's vision that "cluster around" a "Quaker center"; and indeed, even Whitman's basic esthetics are set in a specific Quaker reference.[7]

If we go back to Edwards, and we must, for a rich understanding of New England Transcendentalism, it seems to me worthwhile that we go back to Woolman. I make no claim for Woolman's direct influence on Emerson, Thoreau, or Whitman, although indeed there may have been some. Emerson, through Channing, had been introduced to Woolman's *Journal,* and we have noted his high praise of the *Journal.* And it would seem likely that Whitman was at least familiar with the man who was the great Quaker saint of the preceding century. We should mention, too, that Thoreau's friend, Daniel Ricketson, was a Quaker and a great admirer of Woolman whom he mentions in a letter to Thoreau;[8] it is reasonable, therefore, to suppose that he and Thoreau discussed Woolman. Although we cannot so far speak with certainty of direct influence, I would suggest at the least that Woolman best exemplified those Quaker qualities which touched the thought of Emerson and Whitman, and Thoreau, too, despite his seeming dislike at times of Quakers.

In summary, Emerson, Thoreau, and Whitman believed the intuitive grasp of experience is the highest mode of cognition. They believed that no authority was higher than the "inner law" of self and that the knowledge of greatest value was what Wool-

man calls a "feeling knowledge." There were, of course, significant differences in the nature, degree, and response among them
to these generalized "truths." Emerson's concept of intuition, for
example, may have been far more "inclusive" than Thoreau's or
Whitman's.[9]

None of these three men was essentially and characteristically
a mystic, although there was in each of them a strain of mysticism. They were idealists—they were considerably more Kantian
than Lockeian. As Emerson said in "The Transcendentalist":

> The Idealism of the present day acquired the name of
> Transcendental from the use of that term by Immanuel Kant . . .
> who replied to the skeptical philosophy of Locke, which insisted
> there was nothing in the intellect that was not previously in the
> experience of the senses, by showing that there was a very
> important class of ideas or imperative forms, which did not come
> by experience, but through which experience was acquired; that
> these were intuitions of the mind itself; and he denominated
> them Transcendental forms.

This simplified version of Kantian idealism helps us to understand the fundamental distinction between the idealist and the
mystic, between the Transcendentalist, like Emerson, and the
Quaker, like Woolman. For the Transcendentalist, the mind itself
is active, is "doer." Indeed, the mind creates our world, for the
world is our perception of it. And the transformation of form
between the mind and the world becomes one of the many complex problems with which the philosophizing Transcendentalist
had to deal.

Woolman conceives the mind as "passive." Perception is not
creation. The forms of consciousness are really forms of light.
There is, therefore, no reveling in the self—no details of the "I"
as we find them in Emerson, Thoreau, and Whitman. Emerson's
interest in representative men, Thoreau's insistence on the "I"—
"We commonly do not remember that it is, after all, always the
first person that is speaking"—or Whitman's declaration, "Cama-
rado, this is no book! Who touches this touches a man," are far
removed in spirit and intent from Woolman's work. Woolman
did not wish to present an account of himself: his *Journal* is one
of the most impersonal autobiographies ever written.[10] We sense

continually Woolman's attempt to make the work free from the author. The self, as Woolman says at the end of the *Journal*, must be "kept out."

William James, paraphrasing Robert Louis Stevenson, "To omit is the one art in literature," then quotes Stevenson: " 'If I knew how to omit, I should ask no other knowledge.' " James comments upon this statement:

> And life, when full of disorder and slackness and vague super-fluity, can no more have what we call character than literature can have it under similar conditions. So monasteries and communities of sympathetic devotees open their doors, and in their changeless order, characterized by omissions quite as much as constituted of actions, the holy-minded person finds that inner smoothness and cleanness which it is torture to him to feel violated at every turn by the discordancy and brutality of secular existence.[11]

Part of the inspiration for this observation is derived from Woolman's singularity in wearing undyed clothes. James felt that Woolman was "jarred" to active protest by "the slightest inconsistency between protest and deed." James sees "the craving for moral consistency and purity" that we find in Woolman and others as "the law of omission": "That law which impels the artist to achieve harmony in his composition by simply dropping out whatever jars, or suggests a discord, rules also in the spiritual life."[12]

Woolman, like Thoreau, was an ascetic in his manly attempt to live the hardy life of necessities and in his scorn of ease. Unlike Thoreau, Woolman often carries his asceticism or "omissions" toward a rather grim seriousness that takes away from us moods of spontaneity and joy, that destroys the beauty of device, artifice, and color. Asceticism, however, did not make for monasticism, and Woolman walked right into "the discordancy and brutality of secular existence."

Woolman's belief that the self must be kept out is perhaps the highest "grade," to use James's word, of asceticism. In the law of omission, what could be more final or ultimate than the abnegation of self? This is the nature of Woolman's asceticism, and this particular kind of asceticism sharply distinguishes him from the Transcendentalists. The great thing is that his asceticism, nurtured by piety and attained through quietism, was not marred by psychological perversions or mortifying obsessions: it is fascinating to observe how the fruits of asceticism ripen into social revolution.

Esthetically, the law of omission does effect a lovely and even grand harmony. It fixes the Word at the center of the *Journal*. All waverings and fluctuations of the self, all discord and all torment, are eventually and resolutely absorbed by the overarching, eternal, and silent Word.

So it is that Woolman, a man of perhaps unexceptional literary talent—certainly with much less skill than an Emerson, a Thoreau, or a Whitman— is saved by the "strength and lucidity" of vision that is derived from "the modes of traditional piety." It is no tautology to say the divineness of self is founded in God. More often than not, "divinity" in American and English Romanticism is a philosophical and metaphysical position rather than a theological one.

In Woolman, almost unique among American writers, we find the union of passion and morality rather than the struggle or antagonism of allegiances. We find no lasting disparities between thought and action, between idea and experience. There is always an omission to be made that is of the essence of character, and in a society of superfluity and luxury this kind of ascetic discipline moves us toward the light. Nothing finally dies in the *Journal* for the lines of light are everywhere. They do not filiate with a Rock of Ages, but rather with the stepping stones in a miry place.

## II  *The Reader as Communicant*

*The Journal of John Woolman*, we have said, is in itself a sacramental act. Its concern is not with "effect" but with the motion and reality of the act. And it is necessary that the motion and reality of the act, as Woolman tells us, "arises from heavenly love." In this way the reader of the *Journal* becomes a kind of communicant; and Woolman, a kind of priest. Indeed, without dogma or doctrine, Woolman is liable at times to become the priest of improvisation, but the act always involves the same oblation: every action involves implicity or explicitly the giving of the self to God. This is the mystical temper, and it is in sharp contrast to the Romantic idealism of Whitman who declared in one of his more buoyant moods: "Nothing! Not even God is greater than one's self." The self in Whitman is not oblatory but godlike. Whitman wants to make of us not communicants but striding young gods.

To be communicants is to have lifted from us somewhat our personal responsibilities, our convictions of sin and of moribund realities. Our anxieties are put to rest, and we are made "free." Our "witness" becomes more significant than our acceptance. We are made part of the act by being there, by reading. The effect of the act upon us individually is not an accentuated one. The important thing is the reality and the motion of the act. Thus, we too, however temporary, in the reading move along with Woolman toward an annihilation of the "I." If the purpose of a work is to bear witness to the "light," then stated or unstated, the aim is also to evangelize or to convert. In Whitman, we may or may not be liberated by becoming gods. The way is free, open, and hazardous. Death, however, awaits the gods; and the meaningful questions raised lead to abstractions and ideal values, not to religion.

What we mean to comment upon finally is that the *Journal* is, after all, a Quaker document. It carries the truth for Quakerism: the writer's salvation through acceptance of the teachings of the Quakers. There are no heresies in Woolman's writing, no conflicts with Quaker "testimony." The radicalism of the work is in its complete acceptance of a radical faith, and in its attempt to keep that faith pure. Perhaps we might say "orthodoxy" rather than "radicalism," if the first word did not imply inflexibility. In addition to the list of all the things we have said about the *Journal*, we must also say that it is the highest sort of propaganda. It has come through the early censorship committee to serve the noble Quaker cause.

What saves it from the pitfalls of low propaganda or base sectarianism is in part its sacramental nature which destroys urgencies and enthusiasms. We may participate in Woolman's spiritual voyage without being called upon. What matters is not the proselytizing but the thoughtful narrative with its occasional "feel" for scene and portrait. It is not autobiographical detail and chronology that hold us, not the usual workings of suspense. Woolman created no rich tapestries of scene; but, in a very elementary fashion, his *Journal* is chiefly a series of "movements," the significance of which are refracted through a multiplicity of moral perceptions.

Everything that happens in the *Journal* is of moral import, and almost always the voice of Woolman meditates upon what has taken place. The act becomes static, frozen, because it does not run into other acts. The action and its "chant," whether meditative, elegiac, lyrical, or whatever, has a little of the effect of ritual.

## III *The End of His Pilgrimage*

We have seen that Woolman's essays and *Journal* were the response of a saint to life in the American colonies, a response to his culture, to the central problems of slavery, the Indian, poverty, and war. His response was often antithetical to that of his contemporaries, but history was to vindicate Woolman to show how right he usually was. His central concerns—war, civil rights, poverty—are the three great political, social, and moral concerns of our time. If it is true, as Emerson says in "Self-Reliance," that "your conformity explains nothing," then we may say of Woolman that his nonconformity explained a good deal; and its appeal is to our moment of life and the dimly perceived future.

Woolman's appeal has in it the genius of compassion, a compassion wrung from the agony of his own heart. In the closing days of his life as he lay dying of smallpox in a household in York, Woolman asked that this prayer be taken down: "O Lord my God! the amazing Horrors of Darkness were gath'd around me, and Covered me all over, and I saw no way to go forth. I felt the depth & Extent of the Misery of my fellow Creatures, separated from the Divine Harmony; and it was heavier than I could bear, and I was crushed down under it. I lifted up my hand, and I stretched out my Arm, but there was none to help me; I looked round about, and was amazed in the depths of Misery" (319). The opening lines of the prayer could have come from the lips of the dying Kurtz in Joseph Conrad's *The Heart of Darkness*, for Woolman, too, sensed the life of the dark continents of the universe. There was no way for him to be raised, no support save by God, and the prayer continues, "O Lord! I remembered that thou are Omnipotent; that I called thee Father, and I felt that I loved thee. . . ."

Woolman asked of men what he himself sought all his life: the death of the selfish will. Shortly before his death, Woolman narrated the account of his illness with pleurisy during which he had heard the ominous words: "John Woolman is dead." We must not misunderstand this "death wish" as a kind of decadence. Rather Woolman offers us an idea, and he himself embodied the idea, of man waiting upon God. But the more he traveled, the more he came to see the world as a place "of dangers and difficulties, like a desolate, thorny wilderness." In his account of his sea voyage to England, Woolman wrote, "How lamentable is the present corruption of the world!" (292). The closer he came to "The Divine Harmony," the more clearly he saw man's separation from it.

Indeed, in his last years, he seems to have left somewhat the ways of men as he took on a tortured eccentricity of dress, diet, and manners. Woolman's attempt at absolute purification of his thought and action threatened in the end his bond with humanity; for imperfection is a condition of human life. We cannot, without giving way to the sin of melancholia, trace the source of each article of clothing we wear, of each morsel we eat, of each mode of conveyance by which we travel, to determine if it is any way tainted by men's greed or oppression. Yet, if John Woolman was finally victimized by his agonizingly sensitive temperament, he continued to function with great effectiveness in the final months of his English pilgrimage.

Dr. John Fothergill, the London Quaker, wrote to his brother, Samuel, in America: "John Woolman is solid and weighty in his remarks. I wish he could be cured of some singularities. But his real worth outweighs the trash."[13] Or in a letter to Uriah Woolman, William Hunt writes: "We parted from dear cousin John Woolman two days since. He was then as well as usual. He has great and acceptable service here. The singularity of his appearance is not only strange, but very exercising to many valuable Friends, who have had several opportunities of conference with him. Some are still dissatisfied; others are willing to leave it. The purity of his ministry gains unusual approbation."[14]

It is interesting that at the Yearly Meeting which was already in progress when he arrived in London, the Meeting took its first public notice of slavery, and the Epistle that went forth seems to bear Woolman's influence:

> It likewise appears that the Practice of holding Negroes in oppressive and unnatural Bondage hath been so successfully discouraged by Friends in some of the colonies as to be considerably lessened. We cannot but approve of these salutary Endeavors and earnestly entreat that they may be continued, and thro' the Favour of Divine Providence a Traffick so unmerciful and unjust in its Nature to a Part of our own Species, made equally with ourselves for Immortality, may come to be considered by all in its proper Light, and be utterly abolished, as a Reproach to the Christian Profession.[15]

An account of this meeting is narrated by the poet, Whittier, who vouches for the authenticity of his source. Woolman's singularities dismayed the stateliest board of ministers and elders in all Quakerism. We are given a description of Woolman's dress by one English observer: "a white hat, a coarse raw linen shirt, without anything about the neck, his coat, waistcoat, and breeches of white coarse woolen cloth with wool buttons on, his coat without cuffs, white yarn stockings, and shoes of uncured leather with bands instead of buckles, so that he was all white."[16] The story, as Whittier tells it, has Woolman reaching London while the meeting is in session. He has no time to see to the proprieties of his inelegant dress or of introduction. He simply makes his appearance at the meeting, "late and unannounced."

Although he presented his certification, the fear was that he was one of those "itinerant enthusiasts" from whom the society in its more august phase was now trying to free itself: "And someone remarked that perhaps the stranger Friend might feel that his dedication of himself to this apprehended service was accepted, without further labor, and that he might now feel free to return to his home. John Woolman sat silent for a space, seeking the unerring counsel of Divine Wisdom. He was profoundly affected by the unfavorable reception he met with, and the tears flowed freely." He would not be mortified: deep humility is a bulwark. And after he spoke, he so moved his listeners that the Friend who had spoken against him arose, "confessed his error," and "all doubt was removed; . . . and John Woolman, owned by his brethren, passed on to his work."[17]

At this Yearly Meeting, Woolman's active public life came to a close. In September, he attended the Quarterly Meeting, but he was now fatally ill. To his Friends in America, he left a farewell "Epistle" to be opened and circulated in the event of his death. The Epistle summarizes his beliefs, his principles, his thought. It deals with the state of the church, with self-reform, with the economic situation, with the education of children, with liberty of conscience, with martyrdom, with the fellowship of man. It above all deals with the force of love, with the mortification of the self, of the body, so that finally a seeker may say, "It is no more I that live but Christ that Liveth in me." Along with the Epistle, Woolman left in the hands of his friend, John Pemberton, *The Journal of John Woolman,* also to be published in the event of his death.

CHAPTER **9**

# Values and Influence

W OOLMAN taught school from time to time, and he taught not only the children of Friends but "others" as well. He thought deeply about education. He wrote a *Primer* which went through three editions,[1] and he wrote two brief essays, both entitled, "On Schools." The tenderness he felt toward his young pupils is characterized by such sentiments as: "It is a lovely Sight to behold innocent Children" (391).

## I  *Views on Education*

Woolman felt that education must protect the values of innocence from the enticements of custom. Education was a learning to rely upon one's self, to obey the promptings of one's soul. Nurturing in the child the spirit of love for all creation was a chief end—good penmanship and pious maxims were incidental: "To watch the spirit of Children in school . . . is of greater moment than their improvement in the knowledge of Letters" (429).

He realized a child would learn faster if encouraged "to do Things with a view to get Praise of men," than if he were taught to learn for the grace of his soul (390). But this would encourage the child's conformity to the world. Therefore the teacher must be sensitive, spiritual, "sanctified." The teacher must respond to the "Leadings of Truth within his own soul"; for, if he follows "the Maxims of this World," then he will inevitably teach observance to custom and opinion (391). And parents must be faithful to their children, to the innocence of their minds: therefore they must be willing to pay more than they do for education, willing to pay the kind of wages that would make of teaching a livelihood and a profession. When teachers tutor too many pupils in order to support themselves, the situation is not only damaging to the pupil because he doesn't receive the personal attention he should, but it is also damaging to the pupil because of the effects of overwork on the teacher. A teacher must have ample time for reflection, for his own spiritual development. If overburdened with students, a teacher has difficulty in living as a free, spiritual being: the livelihood is drudgery.

Woolman hints at a theory of education that would allow the child to develop according to the child's own "Spirit and Inclinations." This theory, although not developed by Woolman, would seem to follow naturally from his ideal of self-reliance: encouraging the child to follow the promptings of his own soul. But Woolman does not mean the child should be allowed to romp unbridled. One of the sensible benefits of educating children is "to render their Company agreeable to us" (392).

As we observed in Woolman's own education and in Barclay's detestation of the learning of the schoolmen and divines, the Quaker was suspicious of intellectualism. Woolman prefixed to his first essay on schools a famous quotation from Mark: "Suffer the little children to come unto me, and forbid them not, for of such is the kingdom of God," and it is to God that one comes to directly in education rightly performed. Woolman saw the universe with a single eye: the light of knowledge is the light of divinity. The principle of education is "the *Principle of Universal Light*" (428). This principle may lead to piety and virtue in men, but we need look no further than at the great intellectual power of the Puritans to understand where the Quakers went astray. As incalculable and as lasting as the humane ideas of the Quakers have been on American thought, it was the Puritans who aggressively stamped their imprint and made of their seal a nation which has not yet recovered from their energy and their influence.

It would be a mistake, however, to admit Woolman's views on education as representative of the whole of Quakerism. Frederick Tolles call it "a hoary legend" to say the Quakers were "uncompromisingly hostile to education and learning." Although George Fox "had fulminated against the universities" and "William Penn had attacked them as 'Signal Places for Idleness, Looseness, Prophaneness, Prodigality, and gross Ignorance'," the Friends in colonial Pennsylvania, although they saw no need for a college, nevertheless "insisted upon an ideal of universal elementary education for their children and maintained a system of public schools said to have been superior to those of Bristol and Norwich in England."[2] In fact, as Tolles points out, there was an "empirical bent" in Quaker education; and the Quakers "tended to render the 'New Philosophy' congenial for them."[3] Still, the fact remains that the Quakers were hostile to the Academy of Philadelphia when it became a college in 1755; and, as Tolles informs us, it was to be another hundred years before Friends saw the need for higher education.[4]

The problem of whether the Quakers were or were not hostile to intellectualism is not nearly so important as what endures from their views on education. A problem in education is, of course, one in values. One critic expresses the problem in a simple, fundamental question, "What is most worth-while in life, and how to go about to achieve it?"[5] A tentative attempt at formulating an answer to this question forms the basis of Frank Davidson's essay, "Three Patterns of Living," in which Davidson discusses three men, each representative of a "pattern of living." These men are Jonathan Edwards, Benjamin Franklin, and John Woolman.

Davidson believes that Edwards offered us mysticism and heaven (although he was no ascetic in "the medieval manner"); Franklin offered us a pattern of living that is utilitarian (but "not basely utilitarian"); and Woolman offered us mystical insight and compassionate humanism. Davidson concludes his essay with a question: "Of these three eighteenth century Americans, two are almost forgotten. In comparison with their well-remembered contemporary, Franklin, do these two in their philosophies have any suggestions for us, equal to or surpassing his, of 'what is most worth-while in life and how to go about to achieve it'?"[6]

Throughout this book, we have compared these three contemporaries, and we found in Woolman the practical humanitarianism of Franklin and the idealism of Edwards. An answer to Frank Davidson's final question would place Woolman and Edwards among those souls who believe values beyond the material ones are "most worth-while in life." Woolman's fulminations against custom and opinion, his insistence that education is most significantly concerned with the state of the soul is an insistence, not parochial, that bifocals, lightning rods, and electric stoves—important as these accomplishments are—cannot produce great men or form the basis for civilized society.

## II *"Clues and Indirections"*

Paul H. Douglas has sought to appraise Franklin and Woolman, to find a balance for the values of each. His view of their legacy is sane and sound:

> Surely Franklin and Woolman were contrasting characters but, in a sense, they were also complementary to each other. For the world desperately needs, even though it will not acknowledge the fact, saints and mystics with their sensitive appreciation of right and wrong and their struggles to put these apprehensions into effect. And woe be it to any society which crushes out or disgraces its spiritual pioneers. But it needs also its sages and its prudent men who, like Franklin, deal in the possible and help in some measure to bring the apprehensions of the saints closer to reality.[7]

This view provides a partial answer to why Franklin is a literary success—and a national hero—and Woolman a literary neglect. The materialist, however rich his humane imagination, however noble his utilitarianism, has carried the day. There has been no contest: the virtue of "use" has trimphed over the virtue of piety. And, since our colonial literature is fundamentally utilitarian rather than belles-lettres, it is easy to see why Franklin shines like a gem and Woolman, if recognizable outside the Quakers, is remembered as a dusty, somewhat curious relic of an age gone by.

Perhaps another reason for the neglect of Woolman scholarship and criticism is the quite simple one that he did not write in Massachusetts. It is perhaps true, as Henry Canby says, that the Quaker heritage "has been more durable as a spiritual influence than the Puritan, and upon our philosophies of living has been only less powerful than Calvinism."[8] The literary influence, though, has been hardly tested. Until the twentieth century, American literature and intellectual life were dominated by New England; and there was a reluctance on the part of literary historians and scholars to admit that work produced outside Massachusetts, or in general New England, could be worth their scrutinization.

The fact is Colonial New England produced no autobiography

the equal of either Franklin's or Woolman's. Moses Coit Tyler, in his classic study of the literature of the Revolution, writes: "It is no slight distinction attaching to American literature for the period of the Revolution, that in a time so often characterized as barren of important literary achievements, were produced two of the most perfect examples of autobiography to be met with in any literature." And Tyler reminds us of William Ellery Channing's pronunciamento that *The Journal of John Woolman* is "beyond comparison the sweetest and purest autobiography in the language."[9] Certainly it is one of the few readable books of the colonial period.

Although we have discussed ideas common to Woolman and to American Transcendentalism, hinted at possible influences, direct and indirect, and discussed the direct influence of Woolman on Dreiser, Canby has other suggestions. He sees the Quakers as a major influence on Franklin's thought.[10] The Quaker influence, Canby believes, is evidenced "in the idyllic letters of Crèvecoeur,"[11] and in "its mystic communions with a God that said Aye or Nay to the heart, in the struggles of Melville with Moby Dick."[12] Of James Fenimore Cooper, Canby writes:

Cooper, in one part of his soul, was and always remained a Quaker. As a Quaker he judged human nature, and created character when he could create at all. To call Cooper the Quaker romanticist is to put too much in a term, but without his Quakerism he would have been much nearer to a merely American Scott. Without this imprint of a peculiar culture he would never have made Natty Bumppo or Long Tom Coffin, never in short have been Cooper. Lounsbury calls him a Puritan, forgetting for the moment that his dislike of New England Yankees was so strong that even Boston biscuits kept him awake at night. He was Puritan when he scolded, but at his moral best a Quaker. The distinction is important.[13]

There is in our literature enough "clues and indirections" to warrant a serious study of the literary influence of the Quakers. Just as we have discerned lines of major development from Benjamin Franklin to Fitzgerald's Jay Gatsby, so may we discover, perhaps, new and significant lines of development from Woolman and the Quakers to Dreiser's Solon Barnes. At present, we may seek the measure of Woolman's achievement by reminding ourselves of the following: The quality of universality is in no way impaired in *The Journal of John Woolman* by obtrusive sectarian partialities. Yet it does what the Quaker journal is supposed to do; it teaches us about Quakerism and how Quakerism in its purest form works in daily life. Its religious value is self-evident. Moreover, as a record of mystical experience it is, I think, the purest we have in American literature. It is of immense value to the philosopher, of course, and as a record of introspection, to the psychologist. It is of importance to histtorians of American literature because of the possible influences of the quality of mysticism upon succeeding writers and because of its comparative value as a good measure for the mystical qualities in other writers. It is of value for the pictures it offers of American life in Woolman's time, for the *Journal* is, among other things, a travel book.

In its economic and political thought, the *Journal* is not without practical and theoretical meaning for present-day social philosophers and political scientists. Certainly in its non-conformist approach to society, fundamental and eternal issues are raised about the relations of the state to the individual conscience and the responsibilities of the citizen to the state. Slavery itself, as we observed, was part of a larger and far reaching economic concern. Mingled with political, social and economic realities are elements of myth and ritual; and we are made aware of the religious (not necessarily theological) temper of the emergent democratic man.

Surely *The Journal of John Woolman* is one of the most important source books we have of the colonial period. But above all it is the beautifully told spiritual experience of an honest man concerned with the motion and reality of action. In a lay world, he found meanings for the qualities of grace; and he has passed them on to our present and largely desacralized age.

# Notes and References

## Chapter One

1. *The Journal of George Fox*, ed. John L. Nickalls (Cambridge, England, 1952), pp. 103-4.

2. Frederick B. Tolles, *Quakers and the Atlantic Culture* (New York, 1960), p. 4.

3. *The Witness of William Penn*, eds. Tolles and Alderfer (New York, 1957), p. 38.

4. See Tolles, *op. cit.*, pp. 3-4, for his discussion of Penn's account of the rise of The Society of Friends.

5. *Ibid.*, p. 4.

6. Horton Davies, *Worship and Theology in England, 1690-1850* (Princeton, 1961), pp. 114-15.

7. Alderfer, *The Witness of William Penn*, p. xxv.

8. *Ibid.*

9. D. Elton Trueblood, *The People Called Quakers* (New York, 1966), p. 63.

10. Joseph Blau, *Men and Movements in American Philosophy* (New York, 1952), p. 41.

11. Henry Gates Townsend, *Philosophical Ideas in the United States* (New York, 1934), p. 43.

12. *Ibid.*

13. Trueblood, *The People Called Quakers*, p. 29.

14. For a discussion of these various sects and their relationships to Quakerism see William C. Braithwaite, *The Beginnings of Quakerism*, revised by Henry J. Cadbury (Cambridge, England, 1961), pp. 4-27.

15. Trueblood, *The People Called Quakers*, p. 38.

16. Robert Barclay, *An Apology for The True Christian Divinity* (New York, 1827), p. 145.

17. Tolles, *Quakers and the Atlantic Culture*, pp. 4-5.

18. *Ibid.*, p. 9.

19. Quoted in Frederick B. Tolles, *Meeting House and Counting House: The Quaker Merchants of Colonial Philadelphia, 1682-1763* (Chapel Hill, 1948), p. 3.

20. *Ibid.*, p. 4.

21. *Ibid.*, p. 45.

22. Edwin Cady, *John Woolman* (New York, 1965), p. 2.

[ 144 ]

# Notes and References

## Chapter Two

1. Quoted in Warren Sweet, *The Story of Religion in America* (New York, 1950), p. 97.

2. See Walter Altman, "John Woolman's Reading" (dissertation, Florida State University, 1957), pp. 208-11, for a discussion of Woolman's use of synonyms for God.

3. Amelia Mott Gummere, *The Journal of John Woolman* (New York, 1922), p. 14.

4. Cady, *Woolman*, p. 49.

5. Gummere, *Journal*, pp. 13-14.

6. Janet Whitney, *John Woolman, Quaker* (London, 1943), p. 34.

7. Quoted in Elbert Russell, *The History of Quakerism* (New York, 1942), p. 158.

8. Tolles, *Meeting House*, p. 140.

9. Whitney, *John Woolman, Quaker*, p. 165.

10. See Gummere, *Journal*, p. 173.

11. William C. Braithwaite, *The Second Period of Quakerism* (London, 1919), p. 351.

## Chapter Three

1. George Macaulay Trevelyan, *Clio, A Muse* (London, 1913), p. 136.

2. Amelia Mott Gummere, "The Early Quakers in New Jersey," in *The Quakers in the American Colonies* ed. Rufus M. Jones (New York, 1962), p. 397.

3. Cady, *Woolman*, p. 68.

4. For a discussion of the relations between Quaker and Presbyterian in America, see Leonard Trinterud, *The Forming of an American Tradition* (Philadelphia, 1949), pp. 232-34.

5. From *The History of the Dividing Line* in *William Byrd of Virginia, The London Diary* (1717-1721) *and Other Writings* eds. Louis B. Wright and Marion Tinling (New York, 1958), pp. 564-65.

6. Whitney, *John Woolman, Quaker*, p. 224.

7. "John Woolman's Journal," *The Writings of John Greenleaf Whittier* (Cambridge, 1889), VII, 329.

8. Whitney, *John Woolman, Quaker*, p. 249.

9. Gummere, *Journal*, p. 97.

10. Sydney V. James, *A People Among Peoples, Quaker Benevolence in Eighteenth-Century America* (Cambridge, 1963), p. 133.

11. See Woolman's letters to Israel Pemberton in Gummere, *Journal,* pp. 348-50.

12. Notes and titles to these authors are found in Gummere: Adanson, p. 366; Bosman, p. 370; Randall, p. 373.

13. Trevelyan, *Clio,* p. 141.

## Chapter Four

1. Quoted in Rayner W. Kesley, *Friends and the Indians, 1655-1917* (Philadelphia, 1917), pp. 19-20.

2. *Ibid.,* pp. 44-45.

3. Quoted in Robert Davidson, *War Comes to Quaker Pennsylvania* (New York, 1957), p. 146.

4. *The Autobiography of Benjamin Franklin* eds. Labaree, Ketcham, Boatfield, and Fineman (New Haven, 1964), pp. 188-89.

5. *Ibid.,* p. 189.

6. Cady, *Woolman,* p. 87.

7. Davidson, *War Comes to Quaker Pennsylvania,* p. 187.

8. Gummere, *Journal,* p. 78.

9. Davidson, *War Comes to Quaker Pennsylvania,* p. 182.

10. Kelsey, *Friends and the Indians,* p. 46.

11. Reginald Reynolds, *The Wisdom of John Woolman* (London, 1948), p. 23.

12. *Ibid.*

13. Cady, in *Woolman,* believes that Altman has placed too much stress on "the mystical tradition" as "a major influence" in Woolman's thought. Amelia Mott Gummere and Rufus Jones, according to Cady, have also stressed too heavily the French Quietist influence (p. 56). I am not arguing that "the mystical tradition" was "a major influence"; rather that "Woolman's mysticism was not wholly untutored." Further, I think the influence of Quietism on Woolman, whatever the sources, or his understanding of them, is apparent in the kind of mysticism Woolman practiced.

14. Rufus Jones, "John Woolman's List of 'Books Lent'," *Bulletin of Friend's Historical Association,* xxi (1942), 72-83.

15. Rufus Jones, "Evidence of the Influence of Quietism on John Woolman," *Friends Intelligencer,* 105 (Third Month 6, 1948), 131.

16. Altman, "John Woolman's Reading," p. 142.

17. Russell, *The History of Quakerism,* p. 229.

18. Jones, "Evidence of the Influence of Quietism," p. 131.

## Notes and References

19. *Ibid.* Quoted in Jones to show how Woolman "tends to unify the divine and the human and to overcome the impasse."

## Chapter Five

1. Aldous Huxley, "Introduction," *The Bhagavad Gita* trans. Swami Prabhavananda and Christopher Isherwood, (Hollywood, 1944), p. 17.

2. Quoted in Jay B. Hubbell, *American Life in Literature* (New York, 1949), I, 87.

3. Huxley, *The Bhagavad Gita,* p. 16.

4. Quoted in Gerhard Friedrich, "Theodore Dreiser's Debt to Woolman's Journal," *American Quarterly,* VII (Winter, 1955), 388.

5. Gummere, *Journal,* p. 134.

6. John E. Jacoby, *Le Mysticisme dans la Pensées Américaine* (Paris, 1931), p. 101. The passage I have translated reads in the original: "Sa façon de traiter le sujet consiste, par suite, surtout en exhortations. Les principes subjacent en sont, en fait, éthiques, non économiques."

7. David Duncan, *John Woolman* (London, 1871), p. 26.

8. Gummere, *Journal,* p. 401.

9. See Bruno Bettelheim, *The Informed Heart* (Glencoe, 1960), pp. 48-52, 134 *et passim.*

10. One of the last things Woolman wrote shortly before his death, was a brief essay, "On Trading in Superfluities." See Gummere, *Journal,* pp. 503-4. Gummere suggests a comparison of this essay with the earlier essay, "Serious Considerations on Trade," pp. 397-401. See also Anon., "Introduction" to the Fabian Society Tract, *A Word of Remembrance and Caution to the Rich* (London, 1898), where the point is emphatically made, "The whole life of Woolman was a protest against superfluities" (p. 4).

11. Woodbridge Riley, "Philosophers and Divines, 1720-1789," *The Cambridge History of American Literature* eds. Trent, Erskine, Sherman, and Van Doren (New York, 1917), I, 87.

12. Anon., *A Word of Remembrance,* p. 2.

13. Among Woolman's last essays is one statement which seems to suggest that Woolman believed in the equal distribution of wealth: "Now to act with integrity, according to that Strength of Mind and Body with which our Creator hath endowed each of us, appears necessary for all, and he who thus stands in the lowest Station in society, appears to be entitled to as comfortable and convenient a

*[ 147 ]*

Living, as he whose Gifts of mind are Greater, and whose Cares are more extensive" (492). Elsewhere, as we see in the text following, are statements that contradict this view, although this may have been his final view.

14. See Gummere, *Journal*, pp. 401-2.

15. "On the Labouring Poor," *Benjamin Franklin, Representative Selections*, eds. Mott & Jorgenson (New York, 1936), p. 336.

16. *Ibid.*, p. 338.

17. *Ibid.*

18. *Ibid.*, pp. 339-40.

19. See Gummere, *Journal*, p. 409, for marginal arithmetical notes by Woolman.

20. "Positions to be Examined, Concerning National Wealth," *Benjamin Franklin*, pp. 346-47.

21. Joseph Dorfman, *The Economic Mind in American Civilization* (New York, 1946), I, 197.

22. Tolles, *Meeting House and Counting House*, p. 85.

23. Dorfman, *The Economic Mind*, p. 192.

24. For the first time by Gummere, *Journal*, pp. 397-401.

25. Dorfman, *The Economic Mind*, p. 180.

### Chapter Six

1. I wish to acknowledge my indebtedness to Jackson I. Cope's excellent study, "Seventeenth-Century Quaker Style," *Publications of the Modern Language Association,* LXXI (September, 1956), 725-54. I owe much to this useful and stimulating essay for an understanding of Quaker style.

2. Max Picard, *Man and Language*, trans. Stanley Godman (Chicago, 1963), p. 31.

3. *Ibid.*, pp. 32-33.

4. Townsend, *Philosophical Ideas*, p. 20.

5. Barclay, *Apology*, p. xii.

6. *Ibid.*, p. xi.

7. *Ibid.*, pp. xi-xii.

8. R. P. Blackmur, *The Lion and the Honeycomb* (New York, 1935), p. 138.

9. See Henry Canby, *Classic Americans* (New York, 1931), where Canby writes "The Puritan leaders regarded their America as a place of preparation for successful dying, and their somewhat tyrannical grip

upon manners and politics was excused by the exigencies of salvation" (p. 28).

10. Louella M. Wright, *The Literary Life of the Early Friends, 1650-1725* (New York, 1932), p. 218.

11. Cope, "Seventeenth-Century Quaker Style," pp. 743-44.

12. *Ibid.*, p. 744.

13. "Stages in Spiritual Development as Recorded in Quaker Journals," *Children of Light* ed. Howard Brinton (New York, 1938), pp. 385-86. See pp. 381-406 for a description of the various stages.

14. Wright, *The Literary Life*, p. 97.

15. Gummere, *Journal*, p. xv.

16. Quoted in Whittier, *Writings*, VIII, 345.

17. *Ibid.*

18. *Ibid.*, p. 344.

19. Janet Whitney, in her edition of *The Journal of John Woolman* (Chicago, 1950), gives this account: "There are three manuscripts of Woolman's main *Journal* extant in his handwriting and sometimes they present alternative readings. The Folio, the one representing Woolman's final version, is in the Historical Society of Pennsylvania. . . . The Friends' Historical Library of Swarthmore College is custodian of two other manuscripts of the *Journal*, one a complete Quarto in Woolman's handwriting, and one a fragmentary Quarto, the earliest in date of them all, but leaving off abruptly at the death of Woolman's sister. Whether there was once a complete set of this particular manuscript, or whether Woolman actually left off writing it at that date and then set to work on the revised version of the Second Quarto, is impossible to tell" (p. xii).

For a further account of manuscripts and editions, see Gummere, *Journal*, pp. iv-xviii and pp. 610-26.

20. Thomas Clarkson, *A Portraiture of Quakerism* (London, 1806), I, 298.

21. *Ibid.*, p. 301. For a summary of the argument, see pp. 299-310.

22. *Ibid.*, pp. 318-19.

23. *Ibid.*, pp. 321-22.

24. *Ibid.*, p. 345. Here Clarkson is criticizing the Quakers: "If . . . they should put an undue estimate upon language, so as to consider it as a criterion of religious purity, they may be encouraging the growth of hypocrisy within their own precincts."

25. *Ibid.*, pp. 346-47.

26. Russell, *The History of Quakerism*, p. 237.

27. Jones, "Evidence of the Influence of Quietism," p. 131.

28. Altman, "John Woolman's Reading," p. 204.

29. Reynolds, *The Wisdom of John Woolman*, p. 47.

30. See Altman, "John Woolman's Reading," pp. 204-7.

31. *Ibid.*, pp. 218-19.

32. *Ibid.*, p. 240.

33. *Ibid.*, p. 122.

## Chapter Seven

1. *The Journal of John Woolman*, ed. Frederick B. Tolles (New York, 1961), pp. 90-91.

2. Canby, *Classic Americans*, p. 114.

3. See Paul Tillich, "The Word of God," *Language: An Enquiry Into Its Meaning and Function* ed. Ruth Nanda Anshen (New York, 1957), pp. 122-33.

4. See Whittier's reference to Woolman and Augustine, *Writings*, VII, 355-56, and R. P. Blackmur's discussion of St. Augustine and "the rhythm existing in silence," in "The Language of Silence," *Language: An Enquiry Into Its Meaning and Function*, 134-52.

5. Canby, *Classic Americans*, p. 30.

6. My view differs somewhat from Canby's. Canby writes, "Woolman belongs in literature with those sweet-spirited Anglicans of the seventeenth century, Herbert and Vaughan and Jeremy Taylor, whose radiant spirits clothed themselves in words far richer than he could use, but no more pure" (32).

7. See Perry Miller, *Major Writers of America* (New York, 1962), I, 93.

8. *The Letters of Theodore Dreiser* ed. Robert H. Elias (Philadelphia, 1959), III, 822.

9. Quoted in Friedrich, "Theodore Dreiser's Debt to Woolman's *Journal*," p. 388.

10. Theodore Dreiser, ed., *The Living Thoughts of Thoreau* (New York, 1939), p. 9.

11. *Ibid.*, p. 8.

12. *The Letters*, III, 834.

13. Gummere, *The Journal*, p. ix.

14. Friedrich, "Theodore Dreiser's Debt to Woolman's *Journal*," p. 390.

15. F. O. Matthiessen, *Theodore Dreiser* (New York, 1951), p. 243.

16. Sidney Richman, "Theodore Dreiser's *The Bulwark:* A Final Resolution," *American Literature*, XXXIV (May, 1962), 235.

## Chapter Eight

1. See Sherman Paul, *The Shores of America: Thoreau's Inward Exploration* (Urbana, 1958): "And for Thoreau, finally, the symbol of this transformation [rebirth] was not the butterfly which the logic of his metaphors demanded, but the hawk, which sported alone in the morning air with 'proud reliance'—the bird he associated with falconry, nobleness, and poetry and with his own lonely heroism . . ." (351).

2. F. O. Matthiessen, *American Renaissance* (New York, 1960), p. 93.

3. *Ibid.*

4. Paul H. Douglas, "Two Eighteenth Century Philadelphians," *The General Magazine and Historical Chronicle*, LIV (Spring, 1952), 136.

5. Matthiessen, *American Renaissance*, p. 9.

6. *Ibid.*, p. 538.

7. For a discussion of Whitman and Quakerism, see Howard W. Hintz, *The Quaker Influence on American Literature* (New York, 1940), pp. 59-65.

8. See Walter Harding and Carl Bode, eds., *The Correspondence of Henry David Thoreau* (New York, 1958), p. 334.

9. See Matthiessen, *American Renaissance*, p. 42.

10. Gummere, *Journal*, p. x.

11. William James, *The Varieties of Religious Experience* (London, 1908), p. 296.

12. *Ibid.*

13. Gummere, *Journal*, p. 128.

14. *Ibid.*, p. 132.

15. Quoted in Whitney, *John Woolman, Quaker*, p. 374.

16. *Ibid.*, p. 370.

17. See Tolles, *The Journal*, pp. 207-9.

## Chapter Nine

1. See Gummere, *The Journal*, p. 108.

2. Tolles, *Meeting House and Counting House*, pp. 148-49.

3. *Ibid.*, p. 210.

4. *Ibid.*, p. 151.

5. Quoted in Frank Davidson, "Three Patterns of Living," *Benjamin Franklin and the American Character* (Boston, 1955), p. 33.

6. *Ibid.*, p. 39.

7. Douglas, "Two Eighteenth Century Philadelphians," p. 138.

8. Canby, *Classic Americans*, p. 29.

9. Moses Coit Tyler, *"The Literary History of the American Revolution* (New York, 1897), II, 339-40.

10. See Canby, *Classic Americans*, pp. 39-42.

11. *Ibid.*, pp. 32-33.

12. *Ibid.*, p. 33.

13. *Ibid.*, pp. 109-10.

# Selected Bibliography

## PRIMARY SOURCES

I have in the Preface stated my reasons for the use of Amelia Mott Gummere, *The Journal and Essays of John Woolman* (New York: The Macmillan Company, 1922) as the basic text for this study. The American Experience Series under the consulting editorship of Henry Bamford Parkes has reprinted the "standard" Whittier edition, *The Journal of John Woolman* (New York: Corinth Books, 1961), with an excellent introduction by Frederick B. Tolles—an edition that is inexpensive and readily available. Janet Whitney, ed., *The Journal of John Woolman* (Chicago: Henry Regnery Company, 1950), has produced the most significant edition since Gummere's. This modernized edition bases its first chapter on the First Quarto MS. Then it follows the Folio MS. It also prints for the first time the Luke Howard MS., which is the second half of the original sea diary (discovered in 1941).

## SECONDARY SOURCES

In this listing, I have included a few selected books that do not treat Woolman directly because they provide background and information necessary for an understanding of Woolman.

ALTMAN, WALTER FORREST. "John Woolman's Reading." Unpublished Ph.D. dissertation, Florida State University, June 1957. A study of the books Woolman read suggests that "he was strongly influenced by the mainstream of European mysticism."

BRINTON, HOWARD H., ed. *Children of Light*. New York: The Macmillan Company, 1938. Three essays of interest in this volume are a psychological study of Woolman based on Kretschmer's bio-types by Catherine Cox Miles, a study of Quaker home life by Israel Grubb, and Brinton's deductive study of form and content in the Quaker journal.

CADY, EDWIN. *John Woolman*. New York: Washington Square Press, 1965. A stimulating, often brilliant analysis of Woolman's ideas and how they relate to an American tradition of radical and libertarian thought.

CANBY, HENRY S. *Classic Americans*. New York: Harcourt, Brace & Company, 1931. Of particular interest because of Canby's emphasis on Quaker thought in colonial literature.

COPE, JACKSON I. "Seventeenth-Century Quaker Style," *Publications of the Modern Language Association,* LXXI (September, 1956), 724-54. The best rhetorical analysis; explains much not only about Quaker style, but also about its general effects on the development of English prose.

DAVIDSON, FRANK. "Three Patterns of Living." *Benjamin Franklin and the American Character.* Ed. Charles L. Sanford. Problems in American Civilization, Amherst College. Boston: D. C. Heath and Company, 1955. Discussion of Edwards, Franklin, and Woolman to determine the "values" of their contribution to "what is most worth-while in life."

DORFMAN, JOSEPH. *The Economic Mind in American Civilization, 1606-1865.* 3 vols. New York: The Viking Press, 1946. Best discussion thus far of Woolman's economic views.

DOUGLAS, PAUL H. "Two Eighteenth Century Philadelphians: Benjamin Franklin and John Woolman," *The General Magazine and Historical Chronicle,* LIV (Spring, 1952), 131-38. A study in contrast: Franklin, the sage; Woolman, the saint.

DRAKE, THOMAS E. *Quakers and Slavery in America.* New Haven: Yale University Press, 1950. Excellent history which takes into account Woolman's anti-slavery work.

DREISER, THEODORE, ed. *The Living Thoughts of Thoreau.* New York: Longmans, Green and Company, 1939. Interesting comparisons of Thoreau and Woolman. Of particular interest because it suggests the nature of Woolman's influence on Dreiser.

————. *The Letters of Theodore Dreiser.* 3 vols. Ed. Robert H. Elias. Philadelphia: University of Pennsylvania Press, 1959. Valuable for Dreiser's views of Quakerism and Woolman.

DUNCAN, DAVID. *John Woolman.* A Paper Read at the Friends' Institute, Manchester. London and Manchester: F. Bowyer Kitto and W. Hale, 1871. General tribute to Woolman; a recapitulation of some of the highlights of his career. Expresses the view that Woolman lived a somewhat narrow and confining life.

FABIAN SOCIETY. *A Word of Remembrance and Caution to the Rich.* London: The Fabian Society, 1898. Slavery was but one part of the labor question. Woolman had a prophetic role in the emergence of modern Socialism.

FRIEDRICH, GERHARD. "Theodore Dreiser's Debt to Woolman's *Journal,*" *American Quarterly,* VII (Winter, 1955), 385-92.

## Selected Bibliography

Traces the development of Dreiser's interest in Woolman's life and writings.

HAYNES, GEORGE E. "John Woolman and the Coming Age," *Friends' Intelligencer*, CIII (Eighth Month, 1946), 487-88. The ways in which Woolman may inspire men to bring about "a creative age."

HINTZ, HOWARD W. *The Quaker Influence in American Literature.* New York: Fleming H. Revell Company, 1940. Contains a short but excellent chapter on Woolman which summarizes his legacy of liberalism and which discusses his qualities as a man, a writer, a Quaker.

JACOBY, JOHN E. *Le Mysticisme dans la Pensées Américaine.* Paris: Les Presses Universitaires de France, 1931. Important study dealing with the nature of Woolman's assimilation of mysticism and Americanism.

JAMES, SYDNEY V. *A People Among Peoples, Quaker Benevolence in Eighteenth-Century America.* Cambridge: Harvard University Press, 1963. Excellent study of the meaning of development of Quaker "charity." Also briefly discusses the anti-slavery work of Woolman and his contemporaries.

JONES, RUFUS M. "Evidence of the Influence of Quietism on John Woolman," *Friends Intelligencer*, CV (Third Month, 1948), 131-32. Suggests Continental influences on Woolman and their effect on his style and thought.

————. Sharpless, Isaac and Amelia M. Gummere. *The Quakers in the American Colonies.* New York: Russell & Russell, Inc., 1962. Essential for understanding Woolman's position in Quaker history. An essay by Gummere discusses his work on behalf of the Negro and the Indian.

KELSEY, RAYNER W. *Friends and the Indians, 1655-1917.* Philadelphia: The Associated Executive Committee of Friends on Indian Affairs, 1917. Woolman's activities may be seen in the light of Kelsey's history of Friends' missionary endeavors with the Indians.

KENT, MURIEL. "John Woolman: Mystic and Reformer," *The Hibbert Journal*, XXVI (1928), 302-13. Interesting commentaries on highlights in Woolman's life which are viewed in relation to his environment and to his acceptance of Quaker "testimony."

LASK, JOHN S. "John Woolman: Crusader for Freedom," *Phylon*, V

(First Quarter, 1944), 30-40. Christian nature of Woolman's "Crusade."

LEVIE, DAGOBERT D. "John Woolman and the Brute Creation," *Friends' Intelligencer,* CV (Fourth Month, 1948), 235-36. Woolman was "one of the earliest propagators of the idea of kindness to animals."

MATTHIESSEN, F. O. *Theodore Dreiser.* New York: William Sloane Associates, 1951. Discussion of Woolman's influence on Dreiser's thought.

MORLEY, F. V. *The Tailor of Mount Holly: John Woolman.* London: Friends Book Centre, 1926. Short, general biographical account with some human interest.

PEARE, CATHERINE OWENS. *John Woolman: Child of Light.* New York: The Vanguard Press, 1954. Simple, interesting biography of Woolman; religious emphasis.

POWYS, LLEWELYN. *Thirteen Worthies.* New York: American Library Service, 1923, Appeal of Woolman's writings as literary rather than as social or religious.

REYNOLDS, REGINALD. *John Woolman and the Twentieth Century.* Pendle Hill Pamphlet Number 96. Wallingford, Pennsylvania, 1956. Woolman's special quality of sensitivity is more important than intelligence or knowledge in human relationships.

————. *The Wisdom of John Woolman. With a Selection from His Writings as a Guide to the Seekers of Today.* London: George Allen & Unwin, 1948. Wise, thoughtful introduction—biographical and critical—to Woolman's writings and their relevance for the twentieth century.

RICHMAN, SIDNEY. "Theodore Dreiser's *The Bulwark:* A Final Resolution," *American Literature,* XXXIV (May, 1962), 229-45. How Woolman influenced Dreiser's philosophical and political thought.

RUSSELL, A. P. *Characteristics.* Boston: Houghton, Mifflin, and Company, 1884. Religious appraisal emphasizing the workable, practicable nature of Woolman's Christianity.

SHARPLESS, ANN. *John Woolman, A Pioneer in Labor Reform.* Philadelphia: The Tract Association of Friends, 1930. To Woolman the desire for wealth leads ultimately to war.

SHORE, W. TEIGNMOUTH. *John Woolman, His Life and Our Times,*

# Selected Bibliography

*Being A Study in Applied Christianity.* London: The Macmillan Company, 1913. Religious biography and appraisal.

SPERRY, WILLARD L. *Strangers and Pilgrims.* Boston: Little, Brown and Company, 1939. Woolman's life and writings are viewed as a study in the ways in which conscience is matured.

TAYLOR, EARNEST E. *The Challenge of John Woolman.* London: Friends Tract Association, 1916. Discusses Woolman's three conflicts: (1) the natural man in conflict with himself; (2) the spirit of self in conflict with the world; (3) the conflict over slavery and the slave trade.

TOLLES, FREDERICK B. "John Woolman's List of Books Lent," *Bulletin of Friends Historical Association,* XXI (1942), 72-81. List of books owned by Woolman and brief discussions on a few of them.

————. *Meeting House and Counting House: The Quaker Merchants of Colonial Philadelphia, 1682-1763.* Chapel Hill: University of North Carolina Press, 1948. Essential for an understanding of the milieu in which Woolman lived.

————. *Quakers and the Atlantic Culture.* New York: The Macmillan Company, 1960. Historical approach to "the relationship of the Society of Friends to its social and intellectual environment" in America.

TREVELYAN, GEORGE MACAULAY. *Clio, A Muse and Other Essays, Literary and Pedestrian.* London: Longmans, Green and Company, 1913. Portrays Woolman as a generative thinker who gave an "impulse to a great current in the world's affairs."

WHITNEY, JANET. *John Woolman, Quaker.* London: George G. Harrap & Co. Ltd., 1943. The best full length biography of Woolman.

WHITTIER, JOHN GREENLEAF. *The Writings of John Greenleaf Whittier.* VII. Ed. Horace E. Scudder. Boston and New York: Houghton, Mifflin Company, 1889. Whittier's famous introduction to his edition of Woolman's *Journal* contains a brief history of Woolman's anti-slavery work.

WILSON, E. C. "John Woolman: A Social Reformer of the Eighteenth Century," *The Economic Review,* XI (April, 1901), 170-89. Woolman attempted to make every branch of labor "educational."

WOODY, THOMAS. *Early Quaker Education in Pennsylvania.* New York: Teachers College, Columbia University, 1920. Summarizes

Woolman's views on education. Woolman urged the education of Negroes and Indians as "a social duty."

WRIGHT, LUELLA M. *The Literary Life of the Early Friends, 1650-1725.* New York: Columbia University Press, 1932. Descriptive analysis of Quaker literature; important for understanding the nature and history of Quaker literary types.

————. "Literature and Education in Early Quakerism." *University of Iowa Humanistic Studies.* Vol. V, No. 2 Iowa City, 1938. Examination of the relation of Quaker education and educational theory to literature and literary practice.

# Index